THUNDERER

THUNDERER

BUILDING A MODEL DREADNOUGHT

WILLIAM MOWLL

Foreword by Simon Stephens

Seaforth
PUBLISHING

Dedicated to Patrick Hills and Charles Warner,
the grandson and great-grandson of Arnold J Hills

Copyright © William Mowll 2010

First published in Great Britain in 2010 by
Seaforth Publishing,
Pen & Sword Books Ltd,
47 Church Street,
Barnsley S70 2AS

www.seaforthpublishing.com

British Library Cataloguing in Publication Data
A catalogue record for this book is available from the British Library

ISBN 978 1 84832 059 8

Title page photograph and those on pages 8–9 and 130–34 © Herb Schmitz

Typeset and designed by Ian Hughes
Printed and bound in China

～ Contents ～

~Acknowledgements~

I should like to thank the following, whose help has been invaluable to me both in the building of this model, and also in the production of this book.

Terence J Brown, former Chairman of West Ham United Football Club plc, who in 2004 commissioned the building of the model for the Club's museum.

Jenny Munroe Collins, Assistant to Richard Durack at Newham Archives, Stratford Library in London, for help with the originals of the Thames Iron Works Gazette and photographic archive.

F Crippen, signwriter, for hand lettering in gilt the information and data on the baseboard.

Malcolm Darch, for his research into the 42ft naval cutter, and being godfather to the model.

Ascannio Giannuzzi, who digitalised the Proxxon milling machine, calibrated the indexing chuck, and came up with the idea of the slitting saw rivet-impressing wheel.

Michael Grimwood, who parted with the garden seat slat made from *Thunderer*'s original teak deck.

John Hamlin, for his collection of battleship postcards.

Richard Judges, who helped set up the new workshop, levelling the concrete base for the lathe.

Michael Maidens, of ConsultaNet Ltd, who in September 2008 rescued two-thirds of the text over twenty-two days, after a total computer failure.

Alistair Malcolm, for introducing me to Michael Grimwood, owner of the garden bench.

Jeremy Nesham, cabinetmaker, who is responsible for the baseboard.

John Peto, my former magazine Sports Editor, for help with researching the two aircraft.

Don Sattin, barge builder and author, who passed on to me his precious stash of boxwood.

Steve Taylor, professional laminator of glassfibre, who has physically assisted and advised me in the use of this material.

Major Guy Gilks, Royal Marine Reserve, for arranging the short act of remembrance aboad USS *Texas*, 11 November 2008.

Charles Warner and Patrick Hills, who have allowed me access to family papers, photographs and other memorabilia relating to Arnold J Hills.

Julian Mannering, my editor at Seaforth, who has given unstinting support for the idea of this book.

Stephanie Rudgard-Redsell, whose scholarly approach to my workshop notes and first rough draft has resulted in the presentation of a polished and properly-structured script.

To my wife Susie who, stoically and heroically, puts up with it all.

William Mowll
June 2009

~Foreword~

It was through the UK National Maritime Museum's educational programmes which began in 1995 that I first met Will Mowll, and read about the work on his model of the SS *Great Britain* and subsequently HMS *Warrior*, on which subjects he has published two books. He very kindly agreed to give a talk about the trials and tribulations of both building and operating large working scale model ships, and ever since that time, he has been a keen supporter and friend of the museum.

The public, regardless of age or gender, have always been fascinated by ship models. Having had the privilege of working with the National Maritime Museum's ship model collection at Greenwich for over thirty years, I am frequently asked why, and for whom, these truly remarkable objects were made. This is the most rewarding aspect of my job, dealing with a whole range of enquiries: historical, technical, advising on research issues, and answering questions from ship-modellers.

The public are also inquisitive to know more about the modelmakers themselves, who have spent so many hours creating a ship in miniature; for an outsider the motivation for this activity is often difficult to fathom. It involves entering into an individual and very private world. With modelmakers who are not working on commission, and where money is not the prime incentive, the choice of subject is likely to have a technical or historical association with a particular ship, as is the case with this book. There can also be a desire for ownership, expressed by the seventeenth-century diarist, Samuel Pepys, who made the following entry in his diary, on 11 August 1660: 'Mr Deane, the assistant [shipwright] at Woolwich came to me … He promises me also a model of a ship, which will please me exceedingly, for I do want one of my own.'

With the addition of HMS *Thunderer* (1911) to the 'Mowll fleet', it is encouraging from a curatorial perspective that Will has put pen to paper, and recorded not only the historical and technical aspects of this dreadnought battleship, but also the human endeavour and ingenuity required to complete such a model.

As a warship, *Thunderer* had a number of notable attributes. She was the largest and last to be built on the Thames, sadly forcing the builders into liquidation, as well as being a pioneer of the Dreyer fire control system, which some would say was the world's first automatic computer, and also Captain Percy Scott's new direction firing system, earning her first place in the shooting trials of 1912.

In a touching and remarkable tribute to the ship, Will has included in the deck planking on his model a sliver of original teak deck plank, liberated from a garden bench which was made from timber recovered from the dismantled ship in 1927. In the age of recycling, this keeps alive a long tradition of using original ship's timbers in the construction of a scale model.

SIMON STEPHENS
Curator, Ship Model and Boat Collections
The National Maritime Museum, Greenwich, London

HMS *Thunderer*

Orion Class: *Orion, Conqueror, Monarch, Thunderer*
Launched: 1911
Dimensions: Length 177.1m/581ft, beam 27m/88ft 6in, draught 7.3m/ 24ft 1in
Displacement: 22,560 tonnes/22,200tons
Main armament: 10 x 340mm/13.5in guns
Secondary armament: 16 x 100mm/4in guns & 3 x 535mm/21in torpedoes
Machinery: 18 boilers, steam turbine on 4 shafts 20,134kW/27,000shp
Speed: 21knots
Complement: 738-752 officers and men

The model: Scale 1:96 (one eighth of an inch to the foot)
Dimensions: Length 6ft 1/2in (1842mm), beam 11in (280mm),
height (keel to truck) 2ft 21/2in (673mm)

CHAPTER 1

~ *History and Background* ~

Introduction

The battleship era from 1860 up until the outbreak of the First World War in 1914 can be summed up in four words: from *Warrior* to *Dreadnought*. HMS *Warrior* (1860) was the first all iron battleship the world had ever seen, and she was built by the Thames Iron Works as the first warship fashioned totally from iron. She may be seen as a live exhibit in Portsmouth, restored in the most beautiful and authentic way as a living tribute to the finest mid-nineteenth-century shipbuilding in the world. HMS *Thunderer* (1911) was the last battleship built by the Thames Iron Works, and was launched from exactly the same slipway, somewhat extended, as her forerunner. During that time, a mere fifty-one years, warships had modernised from being fully-masted sailing ships which carried free-standing weaponry, to vessels whose whole design and purpose was to be an engine of war, capable of destroying an enemy so far distant that they could hardly be seen with the naked eye.

For years I have been fascinated by the emergence of the sailing navy into the era of the iron fighting ship. These new steam-powered vessels were no longer dependent on the vagaries of the weather for their theatres of operation, and no longer struggled with masting systems which interfered with their offensive capability. This period of naval development exactly coincides with the history of the Thames Iron Works.

By 2004, I had built two very large models of HMS *Warrior* at 1:48 scale, one of which is on permanent display beside the prototype at Victory Gate, Portsmouth. A book had also been published in 1997 to accompany the first model. The second model was built as a commission for West Ham United Football Club, intended to be a part of their existing museum of artefacts and memorabilia showing the beginnings of the club's history and its connection with nineteenth-century ship-building. A further commission followed, which would tell the end of the story of this famous yard, in the form of HMS *Thunderer*. This is how I was first introduced to this remarkable vessel, built as the last and, in many ways, the finest of London's ships, but the ship which finally and tragically bankrupted the already-ailing firm.

Thunderer is classified as a super-dreadnought and represents for the scratch-modeller a major challenge on a scale of 1:96. The long journey of my build has been a very exciting one for somebody who is new to twentieth-century warships, because every step of the way has been a small voyage of discovery. A battleship is not only a most complex structure where everything must fit together with great accuracy, but it is also a place where men must live and work together as a team which will be called upon to fight for their country. A model should be a tribute to all this, and a serious model is a reminder of the sacrifices which young men are called upon to make whenever and wherever war is declared. It should also be a salute to the designers, draughtsmen, engineers, tradesmen, craftsmen and builders, who constructed these massive structures, almost literally with their bare hands.

My hope is that the model of *Thunderer*, which has been built with my own bare hands, will give both pleasure and reflection in equal measure, and be a worthy reminder of this vessel's centenary year.

The Thames Iron Works 1846-1912: The Oldest Battleship Builders in the World

By the time Arnold Hills (1857-1927), the Chairman and Managing Director, secured the all-important order for the last battleship to be built on the Thames in 1909, the noble history of the Thames Iron Works was drawing to a close. Hills' public pleading with the First Lord of the Admiralty, Winston Churchill, to give the men of the East End of London a chance to be a part of the arms race for the defence of the realm, was finally and reluctantly acceded to, although Churchill knew that the proposed ship could be built more cheaply at one of the established shipyards in the north of England. The Thames Iron Works, a private shipyard, would also have been expected to quote more competitively than a Royal Naval dockyard in order to secure the contract. In his obituary in the *Evening News* in March 1927, it was reported that Arnold Hills quoted a price £25,000 less than that of any other firm tendering; this added pressure to an already tricky financial situation at the Thames Iron Works.

The plain truth was that London in 1909 was no longer well-placed for obtaining the plethora of raw materials and fittings needed to manufacture and assemble a 22,500-ton super-dreadnought battleship. Coal, iron and steel all had to be delivered to the site, whereas these materials were an integral part of the supply chain connected to shipyards in the north, most notably on the rivers Tyne and Clyde.

What the East End of London did have was a skilled workforce, plenty of proven experience, and across the river from the Thames Iron Works, the former John Penn's Engineering Works at Greenwich, acquired in 1889. Work in the Thames shipyard had diversified greatly since the halcyon days of pure shipbuilding and now included the production of lorries, cars, bridges, lock-gates, and lifeboats. They were also developing, with great excitement, a reliable 60hp touring car. The car was a success, but the tyres were not.

All these projects were attempts to keep full employment at the engineering works. Outwardly, all was well. A handsome new office block had been opened in 1909 on the Essex side of the River Lea, opposite the old Orchard Yard, the former site from which the works had expanded. The order books were far from empty, but a shipyard needs a ship in order to hold its head high.

The Chairman and Managing Director

Arnold Hills had joined the Thames Iron Works in 1880 at the age of twenty-three. He was the third son of Frank Hills, who had amassed a fortune from chemical manufacturing at Deptford. His two brothers had gone into their father's firm, leaving Arnold to manage the interests of the Thames Iron Works, in which his father had gained a controlling interest as the majority shareholder. With no prior knowledge of ship-building, as a very young man he was thrown into the deep end of a most complex construction industry, at the spearhead of all the new technologies of mechanical engineering.

Although he was the third son, Arnold Hills was no pushover. He was an Oxford University championship runner and the possessor of an international cap, having played for England against Scotland. A classical scholar and a modern historian, he was also a vegan and a teetotaller: a formidable young man who, tragically, was to suffer a most debilitating disease which would eventually leave him paralysed during the whole building programme of *Thunderer*. His arthritic condition had reduced him from athlete to helpless cripple, unable even to lift a finger. According to his obituary in the *Times*, despite the severe nature of his rheumatic illness, his mind remained sharp and 'as vigorous and active as ever'.

Although born into riches, Arnold Hills had a

▲The new offices of the Thames Iron Works, 1909.

▶Arnold Hills, c. 1905. Photograph from the private collection of his grandson, Patrick Hills.

Work, Play and the Football Connection

Out of concern for the workers' ultimate well-being flowed a catalogue of his own enthusiasms for sport, cycling, cricket, rowing, amateur dramatics, and the formation of a brass band. Some of these extra-curricular activities might have appealed more to middle management than to riveters and machinists, but for the latter, football league was the new passion. Hills encouraged the formation of the football team, initially titled the Thames Iron Works Football Club, in 1895.

Within their first two years they had entered the FA Cup and the London League, and from this single initiative for Thames Iron Works employees flowed a whole new future, which outlasted the Thames Iron Works into the present day. West Ham United Football Club plc, known today as the Hammers, take their name from the riveting hammers on their official badge, and the tool of their trade, rather than any reference to West or East Ham, and the club has its initial roots in shipbuilding and engineering of the highest skill and order, of which they may be justly proud.

Initially, it was the connection between fitness at

social conscience, coupled with a strong religious belief in practical matters. As a young man, for five years he lived in lodgings alongside the workforce in the East India Dock Road. His motives were sometimes misunderstood, but there is no doubt that he cared deeply about the welfare of his men, and was constantly concerned about the poverty of the area in which they lived.

Labour Relations

At the turn of the new century, labour relations in London's East End were going through difficult times. There was a general feeling of unrest regarding working conditions and pay within the shipyard, sparked off by the Gas Workers' Union in 1889 giving a new confidence to the British Trades Union movement. For Arnold Hills, the issue centred on his claim that he had the right to employ non-union members if he chose to do so. This was fiercely resisted by the shipyard's activist trade union members involved in the different sectors of shipbuilding.

To improve the situation, Arnold Hills introduced what he called a 'Good Fellowship System and Profit Sharing Scheme' so that 'every worker knows that his individual and social rights are absolutely secure': the illuminated citation which enshrined this agreement for the eight hour day is dated 13 November 1894. The scheme included bonuses on top of standard wages, and the care of his workforce. The eight hour day, when other yards were still requiring a ten or twelve hour shift and sweated labour, had implications for profitability which ultimately worked against the interests of the yard.

▲ The citation for the eight hour day.

▲ The Thames Iron Works football club 1896.

A New Battleship for the Thames

The Orion Class Battleship *Thunderer*

The Admiralty requirement was for four battleships to be built. Their names were *Orion*, *Conqueror*, *Monarch*, and *Thunderer*, all to be launched and completed by 1912. All of them were eventually to serve at the Battle of Jutland in 1916, as the Second Battle Squadron (Second Division). In the First Division of the Second Battle Squadron were the four very latest vessels, all classed as improved super-dreadnoughts, namely *King George V*, *Ajax*, *Centurion*, and *Erin*, completed in 1913. These battleships were not designed primarily to be used in the front line of battle. This was the province and territory of the newly-conceived battlecruisers, which were less heavily-protected by armour plating, and designed to move at a faster pace, typically 6 knots above the design speed for an equivalent battleship. *Thunderer*'s top speed as a battleship was 21 knots, whereas her equivalent the *Princess Royal* (1910), a Lion Class battlecruiser, could achieve 27 knots.

work and play which resulted in the formation of the football club, with Hills as prime mover of this initiative. His Achilles heel in this venture was that he did not approve of anyone outside the works being involved with the team. He deeply resented hiring professionals in order to attract larger numbers of supporters, and dissociated himself from the Club when this started to happen. He did, however, maintain a major shareholding in the team out of a basic loyalty to the men, and had in the past always responded to their needs for subsidising the Club. Following the fundamental disagreement about using professional footballers whom he referred to as 'mercenaries', the Club reorganised and changed its name from the Thames Iron Works FC to West Ham United FC in 1900. By 1904 the Club had moved to their present ground in Green Street from the old Memorial Ground at Hermit Road in Canning Town. Interestingly, even today, 'Come on, you Irons!' is still a shout of encouragement you can hear from older supporters in the club stands, and harks back to the days of the shipyard.

▼ The Bobby Moore Stand at West Ham United FC plc.

Pre-Dreadnoughts

The last ships of any size built by the Thames Iron Works were the pre-dreadnoughts HMS *Duncan* and HMS *Cornwallis*, both launched in 1901 at 13,745 tons. HMS *Albion* was finally completed in that same year at a deep-loaded displacement of 14,320 tons. There had been no further orders for battleships for an agonising eight years.

The proposed HMS *Thunderer* at 22,500 tons would be a third heavier than any one of her predecessors launched into the Thames, and 110ft longer than any previously-built battleship from this shipyard. The Thames Iron Works would also be responsible for making the Parsons turbine engines of 27,000 IHP. The Thames Iron Works agreed a price of £1.9m, which was to prove insufficient, but this was the gamble the directors took to keep the works alive. It would be a breathtaking challenge.

▼ The launch of HMS *Thunderer*.

The Great Leviathan

Fifty-three years before the launch of *Thunderer*, Brunel's last great passenger ship PS & SS *Great Eastern* (1858) was a mighty 689ft long, but the displacement tonnage was almost exactly the same as the newly proposed super-dreadnought. The *Great Eastern* was launched sideways into the river from Scott-Russell's yard at Millwall or, more accurately, pushed and pulled into the water with enormous and famous exertions of hydraulic rams and checking chains.

The number one slipway at the Thames Iron Works had been greatly extended for the launch of *Thunderer*, but this was exactly the same slip which had been used for launching her famous elder sister, HMS *Warrior*, fifty-one years previously. HMS *Thunderer* would eventually slide gently into the river Thames at Bow Creek, at the mouth of the River Lea, with great dignity. She was launched by Lady Randall Davidson, wife of the Lord Archbishop of Canterbury. At the same time, the ship was photographed, with much waving of top hats by onlookers, and recorded in early black-and-white motion picture which still survives.

THE SHIPBUILDING DEPARTMENT OF THE THAMES IRON WORKS 1909

On the 7th October, 1909, we received an enquiry from the British Admiralty to submit a tender for the construction and completion of an Armoured Battleship for H.M. Navy, and on the 5th November we sent in our tender. On the 17th December we received a wire from the Admiralty conditionally accepting the same, providing we agreed to carry out various suggestions in connection with the construction, docking, etc., etc. of the vessel. We found no difficulty in this, as the suggestions were all quite practical, with the result that on the 23rd January 1910, our Managing Director instructed us to run up the Union Jack at the head of the slip, and this may be called the commencement of H.M.S. "Thunderer."

Clement Mackrow, N.A., 'Departmental Notes,
Shipbuilding Department'
Thames Iron Works Gazette, Vol No XIII,
February 1911, No 49, p57.

The Importance of Ship Models

The ability to be able to mimic and reflect the original build of a vessel launched many years ago is a prime motivator for a model shipwright. In the United Kingdom we are lucky enough to have a wealth of Admiralty Board models, half-models, block models, and wonderful miniature replicas of all kinds of ships built over the last four hundred years. Some of these were built for decoration purposes only, and some as working examples of what the purchaser was about to buy in full size; others were detailed constructional models, used for measuring plating lines and making other three-dimensional assessments. Before any of these scaled models were created, plans had first to be drawn. Personally speaking, plans are in themselves intrinsically exciting, because they demonstrate how it was in the past, and how it will be in the future. The thrill of being able to turn a set of scale drawings or ship's plans into a three-dimensional object has been an abiding motivation which has stayed with me throughout my experience of constructing model ships over the past forty years. There

is still magic for me involved with turning lines on a piece of paper into an object which will entertain and instruct even the most casual onlooker.

At the same time as studying the plans, the builder will be forced to puzzle and probe every aspect of the vessel's design; this constant investigation is a separate journey from the model-building programme, and will take the serious enquirer to places never imagined at the outset, and in the case of this particular model, to the other side of the world. So there is the bonus of learning ever more, as well as the prize of the completed model at the end.

Plans for the Orion Class of super-dreadnoughts, and in particular for HMS *Thunderer* (1911), are available from the National Maritime Museum. They are produced in several scales, and are classed as builder's plans rather than modelmaker's plans. They are facsimiles of the dockyard plans: in other words, these are the plans which were used for building the prototype, and the dates of various inspections are stamped upon them, as the ship came to completion. In common with all ship's plans, they were liable to alteration and modification, which particularly applied to the early years of any vessel, as usage and experiment demanded.

THE IMPORTANCE OF MODELMAKING

But not for some weeks [from late January 1910] could we really commence work, as the drawings and specifications had to be received from the Admiralty to enable us to begin the laying off on the mould loft and getting the model made, from which the hull-plating, etc., is measured for ordering. In many yards, the hull-plating is ordered from the sheer draught, but we are still conservative enough to believe that the more accurate and economical way is to measure the plates from a small scale model.

Clement Mackrow, N.A., 'Departmental Notes,
Shipbuilding Department'
Thames Iron Works Gazette, Vol No XIII,
February 1911, No 49, p57.

From such a block model, as Thomas and Patterson point out in *Dreadnoughts in Camera* (1998), a complete presentation of the shell plating, frames, strakes, keelsons and side stringers were all drawn and calculated.

The Boardroom Model Collection

There are several black-and-white photographs of the boardroom collection in different rooms, showing full and half-models at various scales adorning the walls in the new 1909 building. This important display was broken up when the works closed in 1912. The Science Museum in London benefited by the acquisition of the 1:48 scale HMS *Warrior* (1860), which I mention as a personal inspiration for me over many years. I have also been privileged to carry out repair work to the Thames Iron Works boardroom models of HMS *Benbow* (1885) and the IJB *Fuji* (1897) from that same collection. The sister model of *Fuji* is part of the National Maritime (Reserve) Collection at Greenwich, which has now been moved to the Historic Dockyard, Chatham, Kent. They, like the Science Museum, took on some of the Thames Iron Works models and half-block models at the time of the works closure.

There is also from that early part of the twentieth century a much published lithograph showing all the ships built by the Thames Iron Works, crammed together like a family tree, depicting every creation from *Warrior* (1860) to the battleship HMS *Duncan* (1901).

▲ The boardroom collection of models – HMS *Warrior* (1860) model on right-hand side of room.

▼ The Thames Iron Works family tree of vessels built 1860-1902. Print by Johnson and Logan entitled 'Britain's Empire on the Sea' (c.1900), Portsmouth City Museum.

CHAPTER 2
∼ *The Building Programme* ∼

Plans and Scale

The plans service of the National Maritime Museum at Greenwich, in the United Kingdom, carry plans for the vast majority of modern British warships from the museum archive. Many of these plans are to a scale of 1/4in to the foot, or 1:48, which for most people is way too big for a model battleship. In some cases there are rigging plans drawn to a smaller scale, but in order to reduce ship's plans, it is necessary to find out where, in your locality, architects and others have their plans enlarged or reduced. This sort of work is beyond the ability of an ordinary photocopier. If you can possibly afford to have two copies made, one set can be pasted down onto boards, and the other kept for incidental photocopying during the build. These plans are not cheap but they are, of course, historical documents of a very important kind, and one cannot help having great admiration for the teams of draughtsmen who originally drew them up.

The *Thunderer* model is built on a scale of 1:96, or 1/8in to the foot, which produces a finished model length of just over 6ft 1/2in overall, not including the overhang of the ensign at the stern. The plans were all reduced to half size, on the same copying machine, at the same time, and on the same settings. This is important, because it means that there is no variation between the plans themselves. The builder needs the body plan, the profile plan and the elevation, as a bare minimum. This gives the three dimensions which are vital. The rigging plan can always be at a smaller scale, and is usually drawn as such. Because these plans have been used for building the ship in full size, they are highly detailed and require a great deal of attention and study from the model builder at the outset, and probably at a time when he or she is longing to make a physical start on the model. But in the beginning, study of the plans is absolutely vital, particularly with reference to the keel and frame positions.

▼ The Thames Iron Works drawing office.

Pasting Down the Plans

The first step in the major build is to photocopy images of the body plan in preparation for pasting these down along the vertical line to the keel. Some people are of the opinion that pasting down plans will distort the measurements, by virtue of the expansion of the paper onto the board when it becomes wet, and the subsequent shrinkage when it then dries out. My response to this is that, unless you are a qualified draughtsman, this distortion is unlikely to be of consequence to a finished model, particularly if the pasting is done with the same paste mix onto the same quality of board. The use of MDF (medium density fibreboard) has caused me no apparent problems, and with an ordinary mix of wallpaper paste, I cannot detect any serious loss of accuracy. However, I would encourage the help of an assistant in laying out the plans onto the backing boards, because it is physically difficult to do with long lengths of paper, and it is very helpful if the plans are laid squarely to the backing board. Another tip is to have the backing boards cut to the same length and width, so that when they are on display, or not required at that moment, they can be easily substituted or swapped over, using the same hanging hooks or shelf. In order to prevent warping, the boards must also be pasted on the reverse side: newspaper is perfectly adequate for this purpose.

The Building Board

As well as the MDF backing sheets for the pasted plans, there will also be a need for a plastic-coated baseboard with a single groove machined down the middle of it, to match the width of the false keel. This could also be done with blocks, and follows the idea of keeping the keel straight during the early building process. It is one of the key principles of shipbuilding to try and ensure that the keel member remains straight and true, and there is every reason to watch out for the apparent determination of this member to distort or wander due to the many strains which subsequent planking will place upon it.

The groove can be made with either a rise-and-fall table saw or, as I did, with a radial arm saw, which is simply a suspended circular saw running in overhead rails. This process does not require sophisticated machinery – it can be achieved with a tenon saw, a sharp chisel, and patience.

The building board will subsequently be marked up with an engineer's set square for the locations of the bulkhead and frame positions. These are vital to the accuracy of the hull, and the clarity of a white plastic-coated board is ideal for the work. This is normally sold as shelving material, called Contiplas in the UK.

▼ The hull in three dimensions: note the pasted-down plan view on MDF board behind the model. Also the white plastic-covered building board, marked up with the frame numbers, transcribed from the plan view. Note also the keel slot sawn down the centre of the Contiplas board, which has held the keel straight in the early part of the hull-building programme.

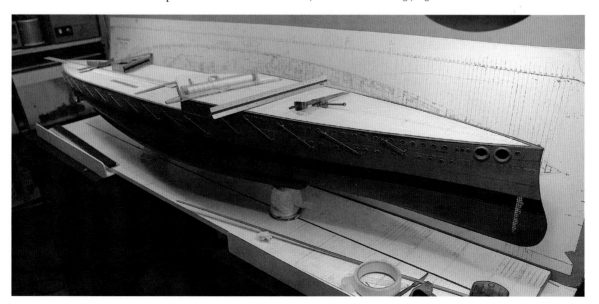

THE BUILDING OF *THUNDERER* BEGINS

In view of the greater breadth of the modern battleship over those of five or six years ago, we had to increase the width of our launching ways, which entailed driving some 600 pitch-pine piles varying in length from 25 to 70 feet. These all had to be cut down, tenoned, and the ground ways fitted to them to carry the launching ways. The keel-blocks then had to be laid, and on 13th April, 1910, the first keel-plate was laid and riveted by Mrs. Arnold F. Hills. This may be taken as the official commencement of the real building of the ship. From this day forward, our great effort has been to carry the work on with all speed, and from commencing with, say, 100 men, we have gradually worked up week by week till now some 3,000 are employed.

Clement Mackrow, N.A., 'Departmental Notes, Shipbuilding Department'
Thames Iron Works Gazette, Vol No XIII, February 1911, No 49, p57.

▲ Mrs Arnold Hills, laying the keel-plate on 13 April, 1910.

The Body Plan Squares

The building programme of the model ship begins with photocopying the bulkheads of the hull. You will need to have sufficient photocopies for the bulkhead frame profiles and what are called the half-frames which appear at the extremes of the vessel. Typically, there are twenty-five of these in total, but it is always worth having a few extra squares to hand in case of mistakes. Just to be clear about the terminology, the bulkhead frames are part of the body lines of the total ship, and they are the prominent ones seen on the end view of any ship's plans shown as half the profile, fore and aft.

▲ The photocopied images pasted onto the upper squares. The vertical line of the body line plan coincides with the sawn edge of the square, for good registration into the slots of the backbone of the full keel piece.

The ship's frames are more numerous, and typically are spaced approximately two feet apart, with *Thunderer* having a total of 250 of these.

The Sawn Squares

You now need to mark up, in order, all the photocopied bulkhead frames and half-frames with a coloured pen around the profile to be sawn, and then number them. These photocopied images, like the plans, will need to be pasted down carefully onto 4mm plywood sawn squares, with particular attention being given to the vertical edge which registers from the keel at 90 degrees. This vertical line of the photocopied image must coincide with the sawn edge of the square.

You will need twice as many sawn squares of plywood as photocopies, because the next move is to partner the photocopied squares with a separate blank square, set beneath it and dowelled to it. Dowelling these pairs of sawn squares together with barbecue skewers, which are cheap and widely available, ensures that the frames cannot move during the sawing and machining process.

The most efficient way of marking the lines is to follow, perhaps an inch or so, on the inside of the profile line. The skewers or dowels need to be a push fit, so measure the diameter of the drill to the dowel in a piece of scrap wood before beginning. The point of all this preparation is that the frames, when they have been

▲ A square of 4mm ply with body line plan pasted to it. Underneath is matching second 4mm square which is dowelled to it. These dowels are just visible on the inside of the red cut line, approximately half an inch or so, following the curvature of the frame. The frame has been highlighted for the band saw cut line, just wide of frame line no. 19.

cut and matched, will then accurately locate at the top and the bottom of the vertical groove of the full keel piece. This will ensure that the profile lines of the hull are correctly positioned to give a fair line to the full length of the vessel. It all has to be very carefully done at the outset, and it takes much longer to finish than is first imagined, but any deviation will immediately show when the hull comes to be planked up. Patience and care at this critical stage of the build will eventually, I promise you, be repaid in full.

Latterly, I have taken to making plank-on-frame ship models using what I will call the 'aircraft fuselage' method. Using good quality resin-bonded mahogany three-ply (4mm), I slot the bulkhead frames into a central member, which I call the full keel member, sawing slots in it on the stations of the bulkhead frames top and bottom, registered at 90

degrees to the keel. This way I am assured that they are machined with acceptable accuracy. I also cut out the centre of the full keel piece at this stage, for reasons which will become apparent later, to do with not having to use pins or nails in the hull construction. This principle of making model hulls can apply to sizes of miniature hulls down to four inches or so, which is the smallest I have attempted. I want to emphasise that you do not need a radial-arm saw for this – it can be done with a tenon saw, or in the smaller sizes just using the saw kerf alone. What the method does achieve is a guaranteed accuracy of the frame alignment, top and bottom, and the all-important knowledge that your frames are set squarely to the keel.

The Bulkhead Frames
A sander was used to sand the bulkhead to the given line of the hull profile. A relief angle will need to be made with a rasp or a sander at both the fore and aft end of the extreme planking where the curvature of the hull demands. A bobbin sander is a useful attachment, but should be used with caution; a better tool is the round-faced spokeshave.

▲ The full keel piece. This is the back bone to which all the bulkhead frames will be attached. The centre of it has been cut out. Note that the keel has extra depth to it, called the false keel, so that it will fit into the sawn groove of the building board and be kept straight.

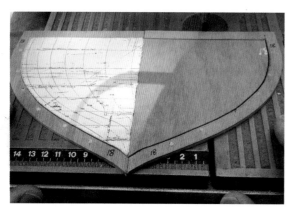

▲ Frame no. 18 opened up in the form of a book leaf. Note how the vertical line of the body plan is exactly on centre for the keel line. Note also the line of dowels which have held the two halves together during the bandsawing process.

▶ Improvised compass follower, marking out the inner cutting line on frame no. 4.

▲ Using the linisher to sand off to the exact outer profile line on frame no. 7.

Bookleafing

Cutting out the inside of the frame is not so critical as the outer edge, but it is still worth doing with care. I use a slightly altered compass as an edge follower, set at approximately half an inch for the inside cut line. Engineers use a lovely tool named an 'odd leg Jenny' for scribing metal, but the compass will suffice perfectly well for this procedure, and a fibre tip pen leaves a clearer cutting line.

The frames can then be bandsawn into shape on the inside edge, the dowels cut through, and opened in the style of a bookleaf to reveal its matching pair. On account of the 4mm thickness of the full keel piece,

▲ Total assembly of frames with the outer and inner profiles cut, but not yet separated from each other. This gives the body line of the ship in three dimensions, the aft part on the left of the picture, the fore portion of the ship on the right.

into which the upright slots have been cut on either side, 2mm from each frame is removed, otherwise the dimensions of breadth would not be adjusted. The frames then have the thickness of the central core of material left in the full framing piece removed by sanding, so that they will perfectly match the profile of the ship's hull.

The Fuselage Method

With the plastic-coated building board under the full keel piece lying absolutely flat on the table beneath, the model goes into three dimensions under controlled

▼ The bulkhead frames are now set up on the building board, into the machined slots, with engineer's set square and a heavy block of steel on the opposite side.

conditions. That is to say, each portside bulkhead frame is laid into the presawn slot at 90 degrees to the keel and is also positioned at 90 degrees in the vertical. Notice at this early stage the importance of the extension of the false keel member, which will slide into the baseboard slot, sawn to hold the whole flimsy structure in a straight line.

Adding the starboard frames to the other half of the hull is relatively easy, but in order not to distort the hull, the slot has to be an easy rather than a tight fit. A slight chamfering is all that is required. The adhesive being used is an aliphatic glue called Titebond, but any good modern wood glue will suffice. In this early stage I managed to snap off the three sternmost frames. This is particularly easy to do when clothing catches on open frames with no topstrake in place.

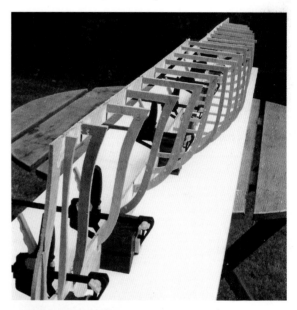

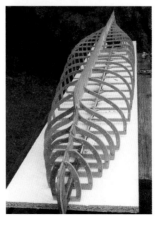

▲ The fuselage method: all the frames on the port side set up and the false keel running in the baseboard slot, ensuring that the keel will be kept straight.

◀ Starboard frames are now in place, giving the total bone structure and shape of the hull, looking forward from the aft end.

Boat Deck Bulwark

The necessary addition of the rounded V-shaped bulwark on the aft wall of the boat deck was fashioned using a technique of wrapping three-ply timber around a hot copper tube, fired up by a propane torch on a very low light. The plywood needs to be well soaked, preferably for twenty-four hours beforehand, and continuously dipped into a bucket as the process of forming takes place over the spluttering copper tube. Every time the timber dries out it needs another dip in the bucket of water. Copper is the best metal to use for the tubing because it spreads the heat uniformly rather than locally.

I am told that heat-treating wood in this fashion changes the timber's molecular structure; from experience I know that it strengthens rather than weakens timber. This technique is a very ancient one and, once acquired, has many applications in boat-building and will be referred to later. The famous

▼ The aft bulkhead piece being steamed over a hot copper tube. The dunking bucket of water is directly below, but out of sight. The propane gas pipeline is visible leading into the copper tube, but the heat level of the torch is kept on tickover only – as low a heat as possible without losing the flame.

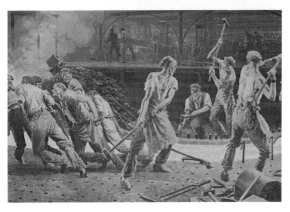

picture of the Thames Iron Works foundry men bending a bracket, with the brute strength required to fashion forged work for metal ships, speaks to me at the deepest level of understanding.

The Hull

Testing the Fair Line of the Hull: The Gunwale Strake

I am never happy with hulls until the frames are supported on their outer edges, and the fair line of the hull is proven. Before this can take place, it is necessary to reinforce the top member of the full keel piece with

▲ The hull is tested for overall accuracy, and the gunwale temporarily set up with clamps and pins.

◄ The foundrymen at the Thames Iron Works bending a bar.

triangular gussets, to make those stations firmer, and set the frames on their top edge at 90 degrees to the keel.

The top strakes of both the fore and aft sections of the hull were the first to be fitted, and removed the danger of accidental injury, as well as satisfactorily providing the outline of the hull. They were pinned using wooden cocktail sticks for dowels into the edges of the frames, these dowels being glued and pushed home making a firm fixture, but as a fallback position they can be easily sawn through if that becomes necessary.

As an encouragement as well as a warning, with ship's hulls and frames there always appears to be one dissenter, one that doesn't quite fit. I cannot believe that this only applies to models, and I am positive that such things had to be dealt with in the builder's yard as well, and this is where ingenuity and experience comes into its own. The model of *Thunderer* was no exception: I cannot now remember which frame it was, but there was certainly one which needed dealing with firmly.

▲ Preparing the slot for the planks to fit into the forefoot of the stem piece. The white line of glue curving round the forward rake will sink invisibly into the fibres of the timber, and provide a stop for the planking to butt up against. Note the use of engineer's callipers as very precise clamps for holding the strip of steamed wood against the edge of the stempost.

The Stem, the Stern, and the Rabbit

Although the stempiece and the sternpiece were cut out as one in the full keel piece, the stem and stern require a rebate to be cut just short of their outer profile, into which the leading edge of the planks will fit, and the tail end of the planks can be faired off at the stern. It is always a tricky fitment to make, and the stempiece rebate is most easily done by steaming a plank's width up the outer edge of the forefoot on the long grain, thus creating a notch into which the planks will fit snugly. When all the planks are fitted, this will give a suitably sharp edge to the stem of the cutwater, which was a particular feature of the super-dreadnought design. The stempiece is similarly treated with the planking neatly faired into the tail of the hull.

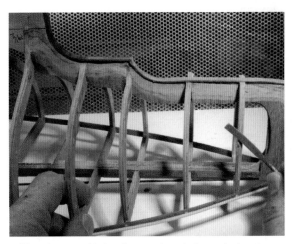

▲ The rebate provided at the stern by a similar method as the stem. A strip of timber following the profile of the aft end, into which the ends of the planks will be faired.

▼ The aft portion of the hull, showing the diminishing lines of the planking towards the sternpost.

The Planing Jig

Initially, there is an absolute requirement for a planing jig to be constructed and, once made, this jig becomes invaluable and allows the builder to control what is happening to the planking lines as the hull is planked up. At the centre of a ship's hull the planks must lie horizontally with the waterline, and at the extremes they will require very accurate width control.

The jig is simply two jaws of a very shallow vice which can come together and clamp two planks as a pair. This allows them to be hand-planed together to make identical partners. My shooting board is a very simple device, but has stood the test of time for both large and small models. It consists of two sheets of aluminium which lock the planks as they slide together. The right-hand jaw has slots cut in it to allow the jaw to slide open and shut, and to be locked down with the thumb screws. The left-hand jaw is screwed to the baseboard. The wooden V-groove on the left-hand side is for mastmaking, and for eighth-squaring mast heels.

▲ The shooting board: two planks are squeezed together before the diminishing planing takes place. Always mark the diminished line with a small pencilled 'V' on both planks when the job is done.

Planking-up

The original dreadnought design has no keel whatsoever, just a bottom line of plating, but as the model construction method is in timber, a traditional form of planking was followed. All planks in boatbuilding will require a diminishing line towards the stem and the stern, and if they are to be applied evenly to each side of the hull, then they need to match one another.

▲ With the hull inverted at the stem, plank no. 3 (not counting the garboard strake) is fitted to frames 2, 3 and 4 and clamped. This is the advantage of frames which have been cut out, rather than left in the solid. No nails or pins are required. Note how the planks have been set into the rebate of the stempiece and lie snugly in the slot provided.

I use mahogany for planking, and because of the size of this model I had the planks presawn for me. Always ask for a sample of the timber to be used before you ask for a whole consignment. Nowadays the quality of some so-called mahogany is very poor. It is quite likely that the longest length which most suppliers have is one metre, and that is long enough to deal with if you are having to clamp them together and plane them, but it does also mean that you need a consistent way of joining them together at the halfway point of the hull.

The Bilge Strakes

The positioning of the bilge strakes gives the eye a very pleasing line to follow, particularly in the aft quarter of the ship's hull. For the first time one can see clearly that this ship's hull shape, with her deadrise severely cut away, is in fact a canoe, and this deliberate design enabled the new dreadnoughts to have a much tighter turning circle and better general manoeuvrability than their immediate predecessors. On the downside, it also accounted for their somewhat uncomfortable sea-keeping qualities, for which they developed a reputation.

▲ Planking out to the bilge strake and the low water level, to ensure a discipline of horizontal lines.

The Linisher

It is not in my nature to be prescriptive about machinery, but I will simply state that I could not build to the standards required without using the belt sander/linisher. It is not a costly machine, but it is the machine tool which is most often switched on and off in my workshop. One of its enormous range of talents is that it can be fixed up with a simple guide-jig to allow for a shallow-angled butt joint, which will straddle the plank across a bulkhead frame for an almost invisible joint. By using two clamps to hold down the guide plank, a constant joint angle can be produced every time. Place the plank against the guide, allow the edge to be sanded by the revolving strap, and repeat the process for the opposite plank coming in at the reversed but identical angle. The angle is immaterial, but the longer the jointed piece can be, so much the better.

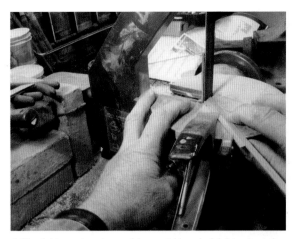

▲ The linisher, set up to provide a matching plank joint automatically. The long plank being machined with my finger on the right hand is guided onto the revolving strap by the short length of plank behind it, temporarily clamped in place on the round table. When reversed, this joint will scarf together with another similarly made one. The angle of the joint is not important, but the shallower (longer) the better. These joints enable the planks to be fixed to a bulkhead from both ends and joined invisibly.

The Garboard Strake

In shipbuilding the garboard strake is the most important plank of all, and probably the most difficult to fit, in that it has to go from the vertical edge of the stempiece to the horizontal plane of the bottom plating, and turn back again for the stempiece at the end of the run. In smaller scale, it is often necessary to wet and steam this plank, but at a length of just under two metres this is not necessary. This plank requires no taper to it but must fit snugly into the rebate on the stem and stern, as well as hugging the length of the keel. The trick is to fit the ends before marking the joint at the centre of the hull.

Once the planks for both sides of the hull are fully ready, then the trouble which has been taken over the preparation of the cut-out frames comes into its own. The planks can simply be clamped into place rather than pinned with nails. The more normal building technique of solid bulkhead frames does not allow this to happen. Not only does this system avoid hammer blows to the hull, which is still in a very fragile state, but it means when it comes to sanding the hull down, there is no interference from pins or brad nails. Never be tempted to plank up unevenly; always apply them to both sides of the hull as a matching pair: this prevents distortion and twist.

The Breadth in the Beam

The planks are glued along their edges with aliphatic glue: one of its properties is to sand back very well. The first two planks against the keel require no taper, but following their fixing into place comes the issue of a flat-bottomed vessel, with a significant beam sharpened to a point at either end. This means that not all the planking in the flat-bottomed portion of the ship's hull will appear at the extreme ends. After plank number three, the next continuous plank running the full length of the hull is number twelve. The planking in between three and twelve provides the hull bottom with its necessary breadth. In full size, this was done by a system of 'trouser-legging' the plates, and will be shown later when the hull is marked up for sheathing in copper plates.

The Whippy Stick or Wooden Spleen

In order to maintain a discipline in the lie of the planks, a decision was made to plate out to the fixed strakes of the bilge, port and starboard. From there, control of the horizontal planking at the low waterline (LWL) and above is much easier to measure and assess.

In very general terms, with a carvel hull, where the planks butt up to one another, the norm will be to taper the plank on one side only, to approximately two-thirds of its width. There will come a point where the curvature of the hull shape reverses, and the plank refuses to lie where it should, whereupon you have to determine whether to taper the other side of the plank or, in some extreme cases, taper both sides. It depends upon the demands of the hull shape, and your best friend is known as 'the whippy stick', or in full size a wooden batten called a spleen – a length of timber with a good deal of flexibility to it.

In practice, this stick will often be one of your unused planks. When matched to the hull the stick will tell you, more by eye, than any measuring instrument, where the fair line of the next plank has to be, and how it may best be shaped. A tip is to mark up fully the taper on each pair of planks with a 'V' to show the swell in the middle of the plank. It is very easy to make a mistake, and fit them the wrong way round, an observation derived from bitter experience.

The Round-Faced Spokeshave

In building a boat hull the constructor will also come across the problem of fitting a long tapering piece in a gap which is apparently almost impossible to fill. This is when you will need to reach for one of the most versatile hand tools known to shipwrights, wheelwrights and the makers of musical instruments, a plane known as a round-faced spokeshave. The convex-curved face of the soleplate of this tool allows the operator to make the longest, thinnest filler pieces imaginable. A hand plane cannot do this, because the flat soleplate does not allow for what is, in effect, the concave line which a spokeshave creates. The secret of this tool is that it can create a very fine and lengthy concave line in timber which, with a super-sharp honed blade, will curl almost to infinity.

Using this technique will repair invisibly those places where the hull makes almost impossible demands on the builder. It is fascinating to see just how far these long fine wedges can be pushed with glue as a lubricant, and to search for them afterwards when the hull is finished. Only the grain of the wood will give them away.

▲ The long tapering piece: the round-faced spokeshave will provide a long taper to the plank and fill the space required for a swell in the hull. The spokeshave is used to prepare the plank, placed on edge, and planed to make the long taper required on one side only. With practice, it is possible to shave a plank almost to infinity, but the blade needs to be finely honed in order to achieve this.

▲ The plank has been pushed into the gap, using adhesive as a lubricant, and has invisibly filled the required space.

The Hull Shape

The dreadnought design has a complex but very beautiful shape, particularly in the forefoot, which mimics an Edwardian ploughshare. The architectural thinking behind this was that water, like earth, has to be parted in order to pass through it with the least resistance, and the forward rake of the bow, with its swollen, half bulkhead frame, would hold the cutwater steady, and prevent too much plunging at the bow. This is a very modern concept, in that the slight swell given by the number one bulkhead frame is a forerunner of the bulb keel fitted to almost all ships now on the high seas.

Dreadnoughts did plunge their noses, as may be seen by many dramatic wartime photographs, but the stem of this ship was an attempt to reach a compromise between a sharp entry to part the waves, and a measure of stability for the remainder of the hull. The flaring of the ship's walls is at its most pronounced between bulkhead frames three and five, and this once again harks back to the top turn of the ploughshare, rolling the displaced water away from the ship's hull in the most efficient manner: flanching is the correct nautical term.

At the stern the hull shape was equally novel. In former, pre-dreadnought, designs, the deadrise, that is to say, the aft end of the keel member, was a significant part of the whole design, and gave a steadying effect to the motion of the vessel passing through water. By virtually doing away with this part of the keel, and placing the four propellers aft the deadrise, this hull could be classed as a powered canoe, with all the advantages of manoeuvrability which that brings. A fighting ship which can zigzag at speed is at a great advantage to one with a slower response to the helm. The last three bulkhead frames lie above the waterline and come to a very graceful conclusion in the crescent-shaped curve of her stern frame.

▲ The hull planked to the low water level. Note that the false keel is still attached and is useful for clamping the hull in a temporary vice.

▼ The tail end.

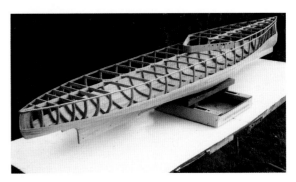

LAYING THE KEEL-PLATE OF THE *THUNDERER*

On the morning of April 16 [sic], 1910 flags were flying over the yard of the Thames Ironworks in honour of the laying of the "THUNDERER's" keel, which ceremony was that day to be performed by Mrs. Arnold Hills. And not the works alone, but all the district showed similar signs of rejoicing at the better times which had returned with the great work which had been entrusted to the yard. Awaiting the arrival of the special train that brought Mr. and Mrs. Hills and their party from Sunningdale, the employees of the company thronged the side of the line, eager to get a glimpse of their chief on this his first return to the scene of his former strenuous activities.

It was a moving thing to witness the spontaneous enthusiasm and expression of hearty welcome, that his arrival called forth; caps were waved and group after group cheered lustily as the carriage passed them on its way to the platform which had been erected to enable Mr. Hills in his bathchair, to be wheeled from the train into the works.

It was obvious that in the minds of all was, not only a great satisfaction at his return but a remembrance of the long illness patiently and bravely borne; and, further, of the ceaseless and undaunted labour of mind the effects of which, radiating from his couch in that quiet room at Sunningdale, had resulted in bringing about those prosperous activities the commencement of which was that day to be celebrated.

The ceremony was coincident with the annual meeting of the shareholders which was held first. Mr. Hills presided and received a warm personal greeting; his remarks respecting the bright prospects of the company giving much satisfaction. A move was then made to a gaily decorated kiosk erected on a temporary staging at the spot where the keel-plate was to be laid, and whence H.M.S. *Warrior*, the first ironclad, was constructed in 1859.

Thames Iron Works Gazette, Vol No XIII, February 1911, No 49, p10.

Laying the keel of *Thunderer* on the extended slip at the Thames Iron Works, 13 April 1910.

Finishing the Hull Planking

It took me four months to reach the stage of sanding back the hull. This is on a basis of working a full eight-hour day once a week. During that process I found it necessary to use another unusual age-old cabinet-maker's tool. A round-faced scraper steel is the only efficient hand tool which can be used in the area of the flared bow at the top of the planking between bulkheads three and five. The requirement is for a tool which can cut predictably into the concave shape, in order to make the planking entirely smooth. Sandpaper and sanding blocks tend to follow the lines they are given, whereas a scraper steel acts like a plane blade on its edge, and depends on what is called the 'hook'. This refers to a slight burr on the edge of the steel, which is what cuts into the timber. Scrapers are lovely, simple tools to use, but depend on the ability of the user to sharpen them skilfully. They do, however, remove timber faster than you think, and great caution needs to be exercised not to overdo the process.

Glassing the Hull

With the hull fully prepared and, considering its size, unbelievably light in weight, the next process is to lay up the interior with glass mat strand. I love and hate glassfibre all at once. It has the properties which most boatbuilders require in full scale and miniature – that is to say, strength and waterproofing, but it stinks to high heaven and leaves a horrible mess. Doing what is required here has nothing to do with the full process of

◄ Model on its beam end, prior to plating up.

making moulds: GRP mouldmaking will be discussed later in connection with the production of gun turrets.

This process of laying two layers of chopped mat strand on the inside of the hull is simply to strengthen and stabilise this hull so that it can never move or split. It is done by preparing chopped mat strand pieces or bandages, and stippling the resin through the cloth with a well-loaded brush. The second layer is to provide a smoother finish to the coarser first layer, and is made of a finer weight of cloth, but the procedure is the same. In the building of *Thunderer*, the extreme of the stem and stern had neat resin poured into the cavities where it was not possible to use cloth.

Never try laying down glassfibre on your own. It needs an assistant, much as any surgeon carrying out an operation needs a team present, and a general tip is to have everything ready and planned before you start. The fact that mine looks so neat is because the process was carried out by a friend who is a professional GRP laminator, whilst I simply took the pictures and held my breath as best I could. Do mask up for this sort of procedure. The chemicals involved have all sorts of warnings which need to be taken seriously. Lungs, like hands and eyes, are very precious and every modern workshop needs a boxful of gloves, eye protectors and masks.

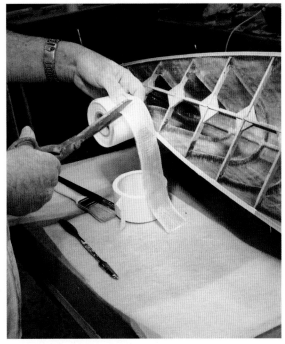

▲ Laying up the glassfibre strips to reinforce the model hull.

▲ Drawing in the vertical frame lines.

Transcription of Frame Lines and Bulkhead Stations

With the hull finished on the interior, the next stage of transcribing can take place. The strict relationship between the hull and the building board begins in earnest from now on. The pencilled 250 stations of the ship's frames are marked on the white baseboard, using an engineer's set square and dividers. The bulkhead frames are also marked on the exterior walls of the ship model. These have then to be transcribed onto the hull, for which it is necessary to make a jig.

In order to be able to draw a perfectly horizontal line on a curved surface, it requires a triangular upright, which will run at 90 degrees along the edge of the building board. The triangle also needs to have the ability to slide towards the hull at the extremes of the vessel, and retract where the hull is at its fullest. The triangle also needs a wide base to make it steady.

In my case, the problem was overcome by an engineer's square, using the edge of the baseboard as a guide, and a slab of steel with a machined face at 90 degrees. The whole conglomeration is simply to provide a flat surface on which a pencil may run freely giving a vertical line from top to bottom. This process of transference takes a long time but is vital for what is to follow.

Metal Plates

Plating-up

Before saying or doing anything further, I must pay tribute to the illustrative work of John Roberts in his book on HMS *Dreadnought*. It is to him alone that I owe the information on the plating lines of this ship, and without his book of scale drawings and illustrations published in 2001, I would have entirely lacked the vital statistics required to proceed with a fully-plated hull. It is of no surprise to me that traditional builder's or boardroom models were never plated, and to be truthful, when the early plating was begun there was a sinking feeling that I was spoiling a highly tactile surface with a lot of nasty riveted plates.

In-and-Out Plating

The hull needed marking out to clarify the plating lines on the ship's bottom and also the five deck levels, including the line of the belted armoured plates, just above and below the waterline. When the full-sized vessel was in wartime service, this was the area where the ship was most vulnerable to torpedo attack, or the deadly floating mines which had been indiscriminately seeded all over the North Sea by the German High Seas Fleet.

▼ Laying down the plating lines on the hull, using John Roberts' research and drawings. Note the system of trouser-legging where the plating expands from the keel to the bilge.

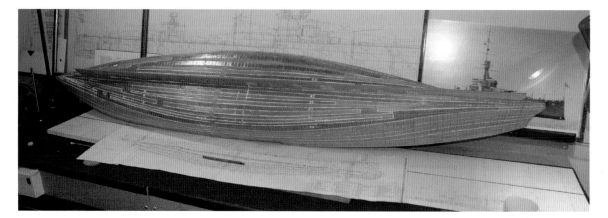

▲ Plate cutting at the Thames Iron Works. Photograph taken for *Pall Mall* magazine by Reginald Haines.

Rivets

At this point it was necessary to decide how best to interpret the external appearance of a warship model of this size and scale. Given the history of the Thames Iron Works, I wanted to demonstrate that this was a riveted ship made from steel with armour plating. The men at the Thames Iron Works had been riveting ships together since the works began in 1857, and it is an interesting historical detail that when the Works football team was founded, the symbol of the crossed riveting hammers was chosen as their logo: so that the team has forever after been known as the 'Hammers'. I also wanted the observer to contemplate the complexity of this method of construction, in a material which is highly resistant, without making the result so fussy that the onlooker was bemused by the detail. I will state boldly, and probably regret it, that it would not be possible to put every rivet into this model at 1:96 scale, nor would it improve the result if you did. What I was aiming for was to gain that particular effect which working in metal, albeit copper, not steel, gives to plating – the very subtle and alluring dishing, which only side light picks up, but which is visible from whatever quarter the ship is viewed.

Light Beams

One needs to know about, and have a great respect for, the way in which light falls on an object. If a model is to be deemed a success, that is to say, both a work of art and a work of science, then it is necessary to pay full attention to the way an object appears to the eye of the onlooker. For an artist with a canvas to fill, the first consideration before all else is what the light is doing to the observed scene. This observation has to be made before either form or content, shape or size, comes into the picture. All modelmakers need to keep this fact at the forefront of their minds, and in this particular case to ponder the issue that perhaps no artist would ever consider, that of detailing all the rivets of a ship to improve the overall effect.

Making an Impression

I used softened copper shim of a thickness (0.1mm) which is reasonable to simulate plating, but it does not allow for a rivet impression which is truly in scale. With this method, it is only possible to create an illusion which will provide an overall effect of construction – one plate laid over another, and in full size, squeezed together with the rivet gun.

Making a line of rivets with an impressing wheel has been going on for a long time in the world of modelmaking. Mine was made following an inspirational conversation I had with an engineer friend, who suggested that different sizes of engineer's slitting saws,

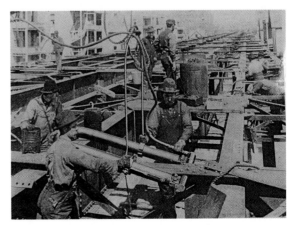

▶ The impressing wheel being used to mark a line of plates from the masking tape pattern.

with their tiny teeth, would give a very closely-pitched line at the same time as dishing the metal, as the rivets expanded the sheet. Experiments proved this to be correct, and I converted a wallpaper roller, of the sort used to seal up the paste line, into

▲ Riveters at the Thames Iron Works using the new pneumatic rivet gun, c.1901.

what is known as a ponce wheel. A second one, with two wheels set in tandem and a very thin washer between them to indicate a separation of the rivet lines, was disappointing, in that it requires a deal of pressure to impress a line of rivets by hand, and the double one came out as a rather pale shadow compared with the single.

Sunken Strakes

The first part of the proceedings was to clad the whole hull in this fashion with the sunken strakes marked with the rivets of the vertical framing lines only – no edge riveting. It was vital to retain the deck level markings on the copper sheathing with the white marker as this took place. Losing these lines would have been a big error. The markings on the hull provided me with the plating lines of 250 frames and the deck levels. The whippy stick was much in evidence at this point, and also the use of the white marker pen. From these marked lines, it was now the task to take small plating patterns from the hull, in reverse because the rivets need to project on the outside face.

For those who may possibly want to try this method, the stages of this procedure are as follows:
- Cut the copper strip into suitable width.

▲ The plating lines marked out on the hull bottom, showing the positions of raised and sunken strakes.

- Masking tape is placed on the hull, sticky side up, held down in place at both ends with tape.
- Cut the butt angle against which the plate is to fit.
- Use the whippy stick and mark the strake with the white liner pen.
- Detach pattern to check fair line against the adjacent plate curvature.
- Mark out with ballpen the frame rivet lines.
- Trim off the bottom line of the plate.
- Tape the copper strip to artboard: duct tape underneath allows for deeper impression.
- Impress the frame rivets only from the reverse side.
- Peel off tape and apply to the hull with resin paste.

Raised Strakes

We now come to the question of the raised strakes, which are more difficult to deal with. Because these strakes show longitudinally, and follow the fair line of the hull, they are ideally made in one long length. This long strip is first marked with the double riveting lines, and then cut to length when fitted to the hull. Their long length means that it is first essential to make a guide or pattern for the impressing wheel to follow. The second row of rivets on the inside of the pattern has to be done freehand, unless you are prepared to make another pattern, which I was not. The whole procedure requires a large flat table covered with a board which has an edge of duct tape, on and through which the rivet wheel can make an impression.

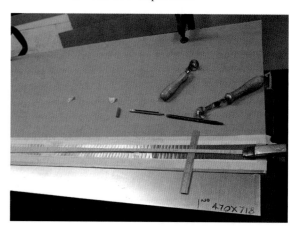

▲ The full length of a raised strake, with a guide pattern laid over it. It has already had the vertical rivets applied, and is being prepared for the impressing wheel to be used along its length, the wheel travelling against the overlaid pattern. Note that the copper strip is laid over some duct tape, in order to improve the impressions of the rivets which impress better into a soft surface.

The procedure for this is as follows:

- Wide masking tape, applied directly to the hull, sticky side down, is marked up with the whippy stick. Apply this tape/pattern to MDF board, which needs to be close at hand.
- Bandsaw the pattern, wide of the line, and finish to it with sander or spokeshave.
- Estimate the width of the copper strip, mindful of the extra curvature of the pattern.
- Wax the bandsaw blade with candle wax to reduce friction.
- Cut the width of copper roll with the bandsaw.
- Reverse the pattern. (You have the image of the sticky side, but for riveting you need it reversed.)
- Secure the pattern down flat with scissor clamps, and mark one edge with the riveting wheel.
- On the opposite side of the pattern, make sure it is all fixed down using tape and clamps with no interference on the run of the impressing wheel.
- Remove the pattern, and tape down the edges to do the inner rivet line by eye.
- Remove the tape from the back of the copper strip and cut it approximately in half, for easier handling.
- Measure the strip directly onto the hull for the vertical intersection of frame lines and mark their position for riveting.
- When fitting to the hull, the extremes of bow and stern need to be tackled first, to get the end of the runs established, then work towards midships.
- Fix in place with resin paste using spatulas.
- The riveting lines on the edges provide a little channel over which the paste must be spread evenly before applying to the hull.
- Do not press the plates down hard. Just allow the paste to emerge at the edges. Secure the plate with masking tape if necessary.
- After the paste has hardened, clean up with cellulose thinners, used very sparingly.

If this all sounds like madness, let me say it took from February 2005 until August of the same year to complete, so the hull was a year in building from start to finish, on the basis of working on it one day per week. I was very glad to reach the next stage, but felt it had all been worth it, changing the look of the model hull into something resembling a metal ship, rather than a wooden one.

The fully-plated hull, minus the raised strakes, which have yet to be applied.

A SHIP OF STEEL

The steel material built into the ship is particularly weighed, and a careful account kept of the amount worked into the ship week by week; this at first was about 50 tons a week, gradually increasing to about 350 tons a week, so that about 9,500 tons will have been worked into the hull. ... H.M.S. "Thunderer," of course, keeps the Works fairly busy, but we must not neglect the other work in hand.

Clement Mackrow, N.A., Departmental Notes,
Shipbuilding Department
Thames Iron Works Gazette, Vol No XIII,
February 1911, No 49, p58.

The Bilge Keels

The convex shape which a hull presents to a bilge keel is not an easy issue to resolve. The bilge keels on this vessel were some of the longest fitted to any warship, some 325ft in length, representing approximately two-thirds of the total hull. This was a serious attempt to recognize that stability would be a big issue with a hull of this shape, without any keel or deadrise in the run at the stern. They are fitted between frames 46 and 210 and, viewed in profile, run from the centre line of A-turret to finish aft of the super-firing turret X.

On the model they were manufactured in three

▲ Applying the bilge keels.

stages. Curvature like this, which is twisting as well as bending, primarily requires a reliable flat surface on which to attach the projected piece, so the first move was to glue and screw a flat section of timber to the hull, in which a longitudinal groove had been sawn, which I will refer to now as the bedplate.

This plank lay easily with the grain running like a conventional board. The next piece of timber (obechi) was fitted into the groove with the timber strake facing at 90 degrees to the bedplate, which greatly increases the resistance of the bend and twist. To deal with this, a series of partial saw-cuts are made to stress-relieve the timber strake, these half-cuts being glued and applied to the bedplate. This treatment reduces timber to a fairly amenable state, with no stresses or strains. To achieve the full width of this bilge keel, a second strake was laid on top of the stress-relieved member and attached by copper wire twists, there being no other way of clamping the timber down. This makes for a massively strong member, which in full size would have given a measure of strength and protection to a part of the ship which was always vulnerable, and always under strain from the racking and twisting forces presented to a hull.

Finishing Touches

Painting the Hull

Colour was my first consideration. Battleship grey is a term which has many possible interpretations: historically, service grey was a heavily-pigmented paint which was expensive to produce, and in the early years of the First World War it was lightened in order to save money.

Given the great variety of car spray paints which are now readily available, in both cellulose and acrylic finish, it is still difficult to find a matt grey finish which has a slight sheen to it. After some searching I settled for an experiment with grey car bumper paint, and although four large cans were purchased at the time, in order that the batch would match, I was to wish that I had bought six, because I ran out of it three years later.

With the interior and the exterior sprayed totally in grey undercoat, the hull bottom had several layers of red oxide applied whilst the top cured off, and the two colours were then screened off with masking tape to apply the black riband which marks the waterline. Paint adheres well to copper, provided it has the surface prepared with a light abrasive.

This all looks and sounds easy enough, but in this

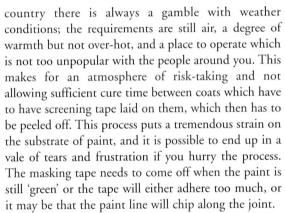

▲ Sprayed grey undercoat. In the background is the ss *Great Britain* model, now on permanent display at Bristol Dockyard in the new David MacGregor library.

▲ Peeling away the masking tape.

country there is always a gamble with weather conditions; the requirements are still air, a degree of warmth but not over-hot, and a place to operate which is not too unpopular with the people around you. This makes for an atmosphere of risk-taking and not allowing sufficient cure time between coats which have to have screening tape laid on them, which then has to be peeled off. This process puts a tremendous strain on the substrate of paint, and it is possible to end up in a vale of tears and frustration if you hurry the process. The masking tape needs to come off when the paint is still 'green' or the tape will either adhere too much, or it may be that the paint line will chip along the joint.

To minimise the many things which can go wrong, it is not a bad idea to make a list of the items to be kept on a separate table close by. These would include paper kitchen roll, some thinners, plenty of precut short lengths of masking tape, spare newspaper, a pair of fine tweezers for picking off the insects, small brushes for repairs, weights to keep flyaway objects from floating off, and so forth. More important than any of that is to have the hull positioned at a comfortable height. Working in backbreaking or neck-straining conditions never improves the result.

Cellulose and acrylic paint make good and lasting contact with copper; brass is another matter, but before any spraying takes place, it is necessary to put on a pair of rubber gloves, and with a cloth, wipe the whole hull over with cellulose thinners. This will make the surface chemically clean, and copper is notorious for collecting grease from hands, and other dirt which will hinder the adhesion of the paint. Whenever you spray, wear a mask, even if it is not a very good one, dedicated to the

work. Once paint is airborne, it will find its way through to your lungs, even if you are working outside.

Spraying paint is a skill all its own. As with all paint, light coats and light strokes will prevent runs – if you do get one, have a cloth soaked in thinners to hand; wipe out the run and then lightly spray over it to keep the coat even. Spray cans do better if they are stored upside down in order to exclude the air space between the jet of the nozzle and the paint, but keep a very fine pin, or some suitably gauged brass wire, soaking in some thinners, to clear the nozzle if and when it becomes blocked. Another little trick is to squirt a little of the pressurised paint into a yoghurt pot, and use a small brush to repair any imperfections. The best tip of all if you are using a spray-gun is to put a small amount of pure thinners into the bottom of the spray can. This gets the jet of air moving into the nozzle and the pigment will not easily block up thereafter.

Display Pillars

It is always difficult to know how best one should display a model ship in the most elegant fashion. There are all sorts of possible ideas involving fancy turning on the lathe, with brass pillars placed at the points of stress; some models in museums depict dolphins, fish and other exotic sea-creatures, but I really wanted a practical solution which would not only not detract from the model, but would also allow for the removal of the hull if that ever became necessary.

The solution came with an unplanned visit to a chandler's, and spotting a full-size yacht ensign staff holder in cast brass: it had that all important nautical look to it. Two of these provided an opportunity to

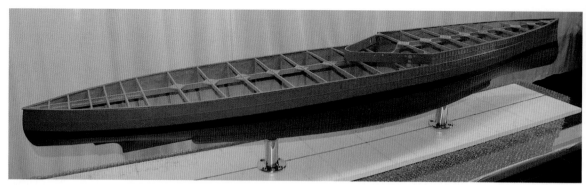

▲ The display pillars giving firm support to the hull. The false keel has been cut away, except in the central portion where it remains.

▼ The launch of HMS *Thunderer*, 1 February 1911. Note that the armour plates are not yet fitted.

make tight-fitting inserts, rather like candles in a candle holder, and retain the false keel between the uprights for greater stability. This means that the model hull is removable from the stand, and no retaining bolts have been used to keep it upright. The keel is an integral part of the model structure, not an item which is simply attached, so it makes a very firm fixture. I later had the ensign staff holders gold-plated at the same time as gilding the propellers, just to keep them looking smart. The plating was done by a local firm of jewellers.

Armouring on the Orion Class

On the black-and-white movie film of the launch of *Thunderer*, I was initially surprised to see a missing line of plating along the waterline. The reason for this was that armoured plating would have added to the strains placed on the launching ways, and it was not necessary to add them until the ship was afloat.

Not being engined either, the hull floated well above the load waterline, but it does look somewhat unfinished. The missing belt was 12in armour plate which, when fitted, ran for sixty per cent of the hull, tapering down to 8in at the ends, but it did not extend to the protection of the steering gear. This vital area was only protected below the waterline. Lighter armoured plating continued upwards to the two decks above, with 9in and 8in plating. The base of the barbettes had 10in to protect their pivotal role. Armour plate was always being improved and experimented upon, but by 1911 the steel being produced by British platemakers originated as a German process developed by Krupps – nickel steel hardened plates which would allegedly break up all the projectiles fired at them, but it was a never-ending competition to try and penetrate the opposition's armour.

Scuttles

One of the characteristics of First World War battleships is their large size of scuttle, often mistakenly referred to as ports. The ports are the square doors which provided much needed ventilation and access points. These can be seen in the open position on the contemporary photographs of the ship. From the point of view of a modelmaker, these piercings need to be done very carefully indeed, not only to have them all exactly in line, but also to prevent tearing the copper sheet.

The gentlest piercing tool for drilling through sheet metal is the cone drill, which steps its way through

▲ Filing in the port doors.

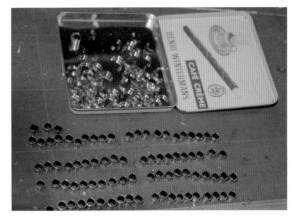

▲ Manufacture of the scuttles and rigols.

without tearing, and that is what was used, followed by sintered diamond files, stroking the metal inwards rather than risking too much pull on the out-stroke, which could have resulted in ripping the metal away from the hull. In practice, the resin paste gave very good adhesion and my concern was unfounded.

Rigols

This is the official name for the eyebrow of round guttering fixed directly above the scuttles. Draining rainwater and sea spray away from the sides of the ship must have been a fruitless task most of the time, but the little rigols are a feature which is missing on many models; they do add character and are not all that difficult to make. There were 83 scuttles cut from 6mm brass tube, all of which required a rigol sited above and attached to them, made by using 3/8in brass bar, which was first bored out and given a rim with a flat D-bit on the material which remained. Once parted off on the lathe they were then cut in half and attached to the slightly projecting scuttle below with an adhesive. You will notice that not all the scuttles are of the same size, particularly towards the bow and stern, and that the ventilation doors have external hinges. In miniature,

these were detailed by metal castings, of which technique there will be more discussion later.

I have never glazed scuttles, believing that depth is very important to models and that glazing spoils the ability of the onlooker to gaze through the hull. It is also important not to enclose completely spaces like hulls. It is much better to allow them to breathe and react to the ambient temperature of the room, avoiding condensation and so forth. Were this to have been a working model, the scuttles would have been filled with pure resin and polished, which is the simplest way of dealing with the issue.

Tipping the Baseboard

Working on the hull sides of any model is greatly assisted by devising a method of angling the baseboard. This was done by creating a separate cradle at both ends of the board and inserting two triangular chocks underneath to provide the angle. It looks dangerous, but means that it is far easier to check the sightlines, and physically to work with drills and files on the hull sides.

▲ Detail of large and small scuttles at the stern.

▲ The model set up on chocks at an angle for ease of manufacture.

CHAPTER 3

∼ *Propulsion, Decks and Funnels* ∼

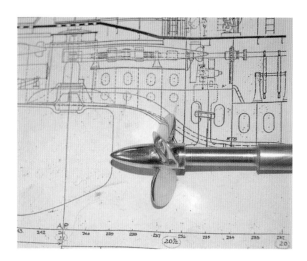

▲ Right-handed bullet-nosed three-bladed turbine propeller against the plan elevation.

Propellers

In isolation, propellers have an intrinsic beauty and fascination because of the hydrodynamic demands placed upon them. They have also been the subject of an enormous amount of experiment, which still continues today. Richard Armstrong, in his book *Powered Ships* (1974), records that in 1836 one of the earliest experimental wooden propellers, designed by Francis Smith (1808-74) on the principle of the Archimedean screw, was accidentally damaged and part of the propeller broken, at which point its performance significantly improved. The new shape was reproduced in metal, and in 1837 the six-ton vessel *Francis Smith* made passage from London to Ramsgate and Folkestone.

The major issue with turbine engines in large vessels is that shaft speed is high, but propellers themselves are at their most efficient running at low revolutions. Cavitation is the name given to the tendency of a propeller to push the water away in a hollow spiral when the shaft speed is too high, causing excessive slippage and inefficiency, so that turbine engines had to be geared down to compensate for this. The propellers also had to be made with a much smaller diameter compared with those required for reciprocating engines.

Manufacture in Miniature

Every now and again there comes a wonderful excuse to spend money on a new machine tool. To make propellers accurately, and on a repetitive basis so that all four are the same, requires the use of an indexing machine, in conjunction with a milling table and a scroll chuck. An indexer is basically a large rotating chuck, connected by gearing to a wheel which has a series of holes into which a detent pin fits, locking a predetermined angle chosen from the 360 degrees of a circle.

In simple terms, if you want the angle of a three-bladed propeller fixed into the propeller boss, you need to index the wheel at 120, 240 and 360 degrees. The root of the blade angle is set up by placing the indexing machine on the milling table, so that when the miller table is wound in, the cutter-bit in the chuck of the overhead milling machine will groove the propeller boss slots out, with a predetermined channel into which the root of the blade will fit. In full size the root of the blade itself is also curved, but at this scale that detail can be lost in the soldering process to follow.

By 1911 the naval pattern of propeller boss with its long bullet-nosed shape had become well-established. On the model of *Thunderer*, at this point I should have centred the cones to the shafts, but I was so concerned with the process of joining the blades to the boss that I overlooked how difficult it would be to bore out the shafts on centre once the blades were attached. Because

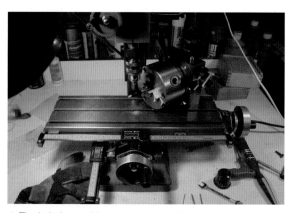

▲ The indexing machine set up on the milling table. No excuses after this purchase.

▲ Close-up of the cutting-bit machining the slot for the root of the blade.

▲ Three blades assembled into their slots. Note that at the top of the picture there are three more with their locating pins inserted.

▲ Blades are being silver-soldered, held in place by the hose clip. Propane gas is necessary to gain sufficient heat for this process.

I made them in the wrong order they presented a difficult task, which was only overcome by centring them in the milling machine, rather than the lathe, and it is not a system that I would recommend. A reminder, perhaps, that with all engineering you always need to consider the order of the process, and not simply the process itself.

Patterns of the blades were drawn up and photocopied onto brass sheet. The roots of the blades were then put in the milling machine facing upwards in the machine vice, bored out on their centre line, and brass locating pins inserted into matching holes in the propeller boss. This system ensured that there could be no escape of the blades during the silver-soldering process. The blades were held in place by using a hose clip on a sacrificial basis, clamping the three blades in place, and allowing the flame from the propane torch to bring the whole assembly to silver-soldering heat for Easiflo 2 flux. This made a smooth joint at the junction of the blades with the boss.

Fettling, Balancing and Polishing

In the softened state which annealing with a hot torch produces, the propeller blades need filing off to the edges, and a small amount of set to the pitch can then be applied by twisting them using flat-nosed pliers, suitably protected in order not to damage the surface.

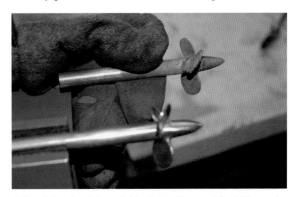

▲ The finished and the unfinished state. The need for fettling and polishing is very apparent from this view.

▲ Lathe-testing the propeller between the chuck and a revolving centre in the tailstock. The D-bit in the tool holder is skimming off the propeller shaft.

▲ Lining up the propellers for the 3 degree shaft angle with lollipop sticks. Note that the propellers are made left-handed and right-handed.

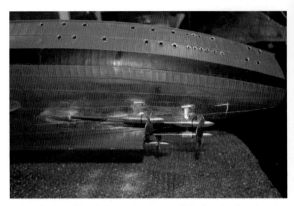

▲ Installation of the A-frame brackets and the bearing housings for the propeller shafts.

Brass in this state is very amenable to being shaped, but will regain its strength once it has been work-hardened. It is not necessary to do this to these blades, but a light hammering would restore the natural strength of the metal should that be a requirement in other circumstances. This work is best done in the lathe, where a close check can be made on their progress and the uniformity of the whole process.

Setting in the Propeller Shafts

With the hull inverted, the really rather tricky job of aligning the four shafts follows on from some freehand boring through the hull, using the extra-long series of fine drill bits. As with all boring-out at shallow angles, the drill bit needs to enter the spot at 90 degrees, and then be brought round to the fine angle required. This initial procedure is best done with a short drill bit which is undersized from the full bore required. This will give a point of entry which will then be accurate, and prevent any wandering of the long and flexible drill tip. It is a good idea to cut a long thin wedge, to give a visual guide to the required angle when boring out.

With longitudinal alignment, the brass tube shafts are then set at the shallow angle of 3 degrees, using nothing more sophisticated than lollipop sticks. The tubes are then set in a resin paste. Were this model to have been fully working, it would be necessary at this point to consider how best to prevent water ingress up the shafts. An O-seal or a gland would need to be fitted in either the shaft boss at the point of entry with the hull, or at the top end of the shaft line.

This all has to be done carefully, but spare a thought for the shipbuilders in full scale, who had to do this job of shaft alignment using a series of discs with a pinprick hole. When all the discs were on centre, and light was visible from one end to the other, the true line of the shaft was physically established.

The Bearing Housings

In support of the shafts, the bearing housings have to be fabricated and set onto the A-frame brackets, and the legs of the frames slotted into the supporting feet. This requires more silver-soldering of the bearings to the apex of the frame, and careful fitting to the hull itself. Because of the rising counter at the stern, the supporting feet of the frames adopt strange angles, which are dictated by the shaft alignment.

The little streamlined bullet shapes of the propeller shaft bosses were made from boxwood, and then mock-riveted in pewter sheet, underlining the point that if you decide to show rivets, you are going to have to show them everywhere in order to be logical.

The Twin Rudders

Successful boring down into the rounded shape of a ship's hull presents issues of accuracy, which need to be carefully thought through before any action takes place. A pillar drill is the ideal, and a small centre drill to lead the way. On this ship the rudders are set on the turn of the plating at exactly the most awkward angle of entry possible. I was not certain that the hull alignment in relation to the pillar drill was in plumb, but there comes a moment when you have to take the plunge and begin, despite your fears that all may not be well.

In full scale these balanced rudders were controlled by screw steering gear which had an advantage over

▲ Bearing housings for the two rudder shafts using a miniature drill stand to assist vertical entry.

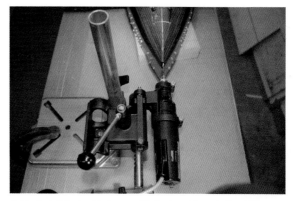

▲ Vertical drill stand being used in horizontal mode for drilling out the stern torpedo tube.

former systems, in that it locked the rudder into position. As Attwood points out in *War-Ships* (1906), this type of gearing could only be used with balanced rudders, but it did prove to be the only source of trouble to affect the original *Dreadnought*'s sea trials in 1906. John Roberts writes in *The Battleship Dreadnought* (2001) that the difficulty was, understandably, hushed up at the time, and had to do with the pivot point of the rudders themselves. It was cured a year later, but nothing stopped her from understeer at speeds below ten knots.

Stern Torpedo Hatch

Almost exactly the same tooling set in the horizontal was required to include the interesting feature of the stern torpedo tube hatch, the exit tube for the 21ft torpedo, submerged just below the waterline. This was the literal sting in the tail of the dreadnought design, but there are no reports of any successful hits to enemy vessels of which I am aware, so there may be a suspicion that this concept was not such a good idea in practice. Side-firing submerged torpedo hatches were also fitted to *Thunderer*, placed between frame numbers 74 and 84 on the platform deck, located in profile slightly aft of B-turret. They were set at an angle of 10 degrees forward of the keel line. Some pre-dreadnoughts had torpedoes in the stem of the ship, but this idea seemed to have gone out of fashion, possibly because of the difficulty of watertight seals, but more likely on account of the streamlining of the cutwater, and the concept that anything which interfered with the action of that knife blade's forward rake might slow down the overall speed of the ship.

▲ Twin rudders in place in line with the inner pair of propeller shafts.

The completed job at the stern shows clearly the relationship between the set of the inner propellers with the rudders and the uninterrupted state of the hull's run astern. This is clear evidence of the ability of this ship design to be able to give a turning circle far superior to any of her predecessors, and convey much of the power thrust and surge at the business end of the turbines.

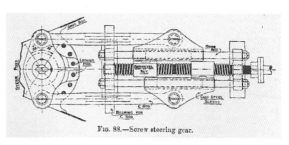

FIG. 88.—Screw steering gear.

▲ Illustration of a non-reversible screw steering gear for a twin rudder installation. Source: Attwood, *War-Ships* (1906).

The Hawse Holes

The external fixings to the forward part of the hull include the three hawse holes, two on the starboard side and a single one portside. They were fabricated from copper tube, using a trick which turns tubing in on itself like a collar. In manufacture, the tubing is brought to cherry red with the propane torch to soften it. It is then applied to the grinder to take off, at sixty degrees or so, the edge of the metal tube, rather like beginning to sharpen a new pencil. It is then flared out with a punch which will 'trumpet' the end. The tubing is then sawn off, so that it now looks like a ring with one edge flared out. The ring is then placed on an anvil with the trumpeted end facing down, and gently hammered, using a soft-headed hammer with a piece of scrap metal to even out the blows. This will, with apparent magic, make the ring curl round on itself and make a collar.

This is a very useful constructional technique which has all sorts of possibilities for making this kind of shape, but it only works well with softened copper, and to a lesser extent with brass. This is how these three collars were made, and they replicate the apparently unnecessarily large outlets of the original. The collars were attached using the technique of a flexible piece of timber, with a centre screw to hold the rings in place whilst the resin cured off.

▲ Twin copper hawse hole collars on the starboard side, fixed with resin paste.

Draught Markings

On the model, the Roman numeral draft markings are by a company called BECC and may be applied with tweezers. They are made from resin, are self-adhesive and very robust, but I did calm the white colour down by using a little painted French button-polish to dull it off. In full size these rather complicated but vital marks were welded onto the ship, so that they could be repainted easily by unskilled labour.

The level gun platform which a battleship provided was vital to the calculations of the gunnery officers when attempting to hit a target ten thousand yards away. The slightest deviation of draught would give false readings, and the draught of a ship under way was constantly changing on account of the coal bunkers and ammunition usage. There were also other considerations and implications on performance related to having the ship well-balanced and trimmed.

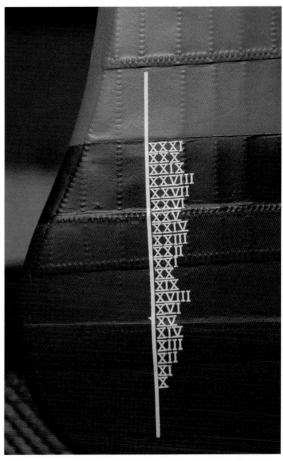

▲ Draught markings applied in traditional Roman numerals.

Torpedo Net Booms

Reminiscent of all battleships of this period are the anti-torpedo net booms which surround two-thirds of the ship, and gave a limited measure of protection to the ship from torpedo attack when in harbour. From dawn to dusk the light always catches these booms, and visually they are a very prominent feature of the hull sides in the early life of this ship. All nets and booms were discarded after the Dardanelles experience in 1915, when it was conclusively proved that they offered insufficient protection against newly-developed and more powerful torpedoes.

The fixtures of the stirrups into the walls of the ship are made like a stud link chain, set into a circular fixing plate. They were made like this in order to allow the knuckle of the pivoting hook free movement when the boom was swung out. The picture shows the spray booth which was used for applying the paint to these detailed fitments, and the stirrups are seen on the wire above the booms.

▲ *Thunderer*, showing how the light catches the torpedo net booms along her hull.

▲ Cardboard spray booth for the booms and stirrups.

The Torpedo Net Boom Keeps

These were similarly detailed from brass box section, cut and soft-soldered onto a turned spigot, and the hinge release mechanism on the side of the keep imitated with short brass wire lengths. The boom, housed inside the box section, has a rounded wooden rest to protect the timber from damage by constant use. In full-size practice, 'Out nets' was a familiar drill, much rehearsed and often carried out in competition with other vessels.

Decks and Decking

Laying the Subdeck

The subdeck gives the final and definitive shape to this ship, and this in its uncluttered form represents a piece of pure sculpture. It is easy to think of many designs of First World War battleships as, frankly, somewhat ugly, but that look derives largely from what was added to the hull as top hamper. It is detail that is often so smothered with canvas dodgers to fend off the cruelties of weather in the North Sea that it is often difficult to see what is ship, and what is weatherproofing. As far as the hull is concerned, in its plain and unadorned state the super-dreadnought is an extremely handsome vessel, and quite possibly beautiful.

Torpedo Net Shelves

This ledge, which dominates the outer profile of the hull, is not difficult to make but it is a challenge to fit. It is fixed alongside the margin plank and waterway of the deck, as well as projecting over the hull sides to avoid snagging on the fittings of the boom keeps. In full-size practice, with the chain netting dripping with seawater, the shelving was a place where rust would never sleep, at

▲ Torpedo net shelf being glued and kept in place with hackle pliers (clips) and pins. The slope's curves are achieved by steaming the wood.

▲ The underside of the shelf, also showing the booms and keeps to advantage.

▼ The sub deck has been laid. It is now time to mark from the plan all the 250 frame stations, in order to have a reference for sighting the decking and superstructure.

a point in the hull structure which posed a real issue for maintenance. In full scale it was perforated with a series of drain holes which were either punched or drilled through the shelf, introducing yet more work for those detailed to paint both the top and the undersides.

At the break in the ship between the fore and aft deck there is a slope which stands slightly proud. To achieve this in timber, the wood needs to be soaked and steamed in order to persuade it into the shape required, using, as a heat source, a thinner gauge of hot copper tube around which to form the tight angles. It would be easier to fabricate this in metal, but the plan was to plate the shelving with pewter sheet, because of pewter's ability to be wrapped around a tight radius. Pewter sheet is a softer metal even than copper, and it was necessary to tuck the metal sheet round and under the shelving, as well as impress it with rivets along the outer edge.

The Subdeck

This is made of 1/16in three-ply birch, which allows for the slight camber to be accommodated without any strains. It is pinned down with cocktail sticks used as dowels into the bulkhead frames and the sides. Screws were not used, as they can interfere with detail yet to be added to the planked deck.

The plan was transcribed to the deck using a long straight rule in conjunction with the engineer's square to mark out the positions of the 250 frames. The centre line was established with taught string running from stem to stern.

Deck Planks and Caulking

The technique for dealing with deck planks is to lay out all the sawn strips together on masking tape and varnish them. This has little or nothing to do with the final finish, but is simply to seal the top face of the planks, which will prevent bleeding from the black ink marker pen. The planks are laid tightly edge to edge onto the tape to stop any varnish seeping into the edges. When the varnish has cured, but before it has hardened off, it is better to separate the planks, or there is a chance that the surface of the varnish will act as glue and you will not be able to get them to part from each other. Likewise, masking tape has a low tack to start off with, but leave it for a week and it will cling with great tenacity and be a nuisance to remove.

▲ Plank strips laid out over masking tape. They are first sanded and varnished, then marked with the caulking felt-tip black marker. To hold the planks steady, they are placed into the grooved strip of wood visible on the front edge of the table, clipped down at the far end.

The plank is treated with a single steady stroke of the marker pen. Mark the plank on one side only; two caulking lines, laid edge to edge, make a line which is too thick and looks overdone. With modelmaking always speak in whispers.

The Barbette Roundels

The linisher was used for preparing the deck roundels at the base of the barbettes. A simple jig involving a plank of wood, a drill bit and a G-clamp will suffice to make a perfect circle against the revolving strap. The inside of the circle has to be cut out with a scroll or jigsaw, but it is the outer circle which needs a perfectly upright edge against which to set the planks. The mahogany in the picture is on the underside of the birch ply, using it as a packing piece to bring the roundel up to the level of the planks.

▲ The barbette roundels being machined against the linisher, using a simple jig of wood below the drill bit. This will give a perfectly round and vertical edge against which to lay planks.

Laying the Decks to the Roundels

There is a principle of construction with the laying of decks which dictates that it is easier to fit planks to existing detail than it is to fit detail into planks after they have been laid. In other words, if there are objects like roundels, edging around the gun housings known as barbettes, lay the projections down first and plank to them and round them, rather than trying to cut details in after the deck is down.

I searched everywhere to find out whether or not the planks were originally joggled into the roundels, as would have been the practice in the old days. The Science Museum model of *Thunderer*'s sister ship HMS *Monarch* (1911) shows a simple butt joint, cut in the round, but as this model depicts a 'drawn' deck, this detail may not be correct. On the other hand, these ships had thick armoured decks beneath them, so were not dependent on supporting the planks at their extremes as with wooden-walled ships. Dreadnoughts were also ships which were built as quickly as possible, and joggling planks is time-consuming. I therefore made the decision to follow what I saw, and butt the planks throughout the ship, whether or not this is what happened in 1911.

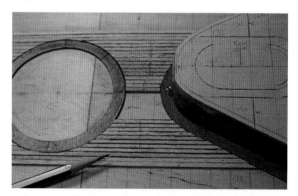

▲ The roundel in place at Q-turret, with planks being laid to it without joggles.

A Very Special Plank

The first plank to be laid on the model deck was done with some ceremony. It is an original piece of timber from the teak deck of HMS *Thunderer* (1911), and it reached me in the form of a wooden slat from a garden seat, complete with a photograph showing the brass plaque of provenance, announcing that it was 'timber taken from HMS *Thunderer*, Jutland 1914-1918'. Carved boldly into the back stretcher of the seat are the words: 'The kiss of the sun for pardon, the song of the

▲ The brass plaque attached to the back of the garden bench.

▲ The citation king plank at the stern of the model.

▲ The bench with the missing slat from which the king plank has been made for the model.

▲ Planing off years of exposure to the elements to reveal the fresh teak beneath.

birds for mirth, / One is closer to God's heart in a garden, than anywhere else on earth.'

The story is that when ships were taken to the breaker's yard under the demands for limitation set out by the Washington Treaty in February 1922, teak from the decks was salvaged and used to keep the much-reduced labour force of dockyard carpenters in work, by the production of rot-proof garden tables and chairs. By pure chance, I discovered that one such garden seat made from *Thunderer*'s deck, complete with a commemorative brass plaque of provenance, had landed up with a family living in Gloucestershire. *Thunderer* survived the Washington Treaty by virtue of being consigned to the status of a seagoing cadet-training ship. She was sold on 10 December 1926, and ran aground en route for Blyth on the Northumberland coastline for breaking up in 1927. All the other Orions were broken up under the terms of the Washington Treaty.

On further investigation, I was astounded to learn that timber from *Thunderer* had outlasted the mother ship for over eighty years. I begged the owner for a piece the size of a matchstick, but he informed me that there was a whole slat which was broken and I was welcome to use it. The relic duly arrived by post, and when the lichen was removed and carefully planed down with just a few strokes, the rich dark brown colour of the teak was revealed once more. This was a thrilling moment for me, and just to complete the story, the owner of the bench, realising for the first time the historical significance of the seat, has had it entirely restored and refurbished.

On the model, this plank carries the citation naming it as original timber, acting as a somewhat out of scale king plank. The lettering is the self-adhesive variety by BECC and is, engagingly, slightly raised in the style of the Royal Navy brass lettering.

Watch Out for Snakes

All planking needs to be measured carefully in width and length, and a watchful eye kept out for any tendency of the plank line to wander off course. Planks need to be laid together, but not with too tight a fit, and they must be ramrod straight. If they start to wander, rip them off, and start again. Remember that they are longitudinal reference points, marking the later positions of the ship's furnishings. As they are gradually covered up, it is necessary to devise ways of retaining the vital frame markings beneath, which will be needed later.

There is no attempt to show the butts or the trenails. Showing these particular details can be a mistake on model ships of this scale, because it is not how a deck appears when you see one in full scale, but this is a controversial area, and people will rightly decide how they like their own model to appear. The deck on this model

▲ Planking the aft deck around the roundels and the aft superstructure, ensuring absolute discipline in the straightness of their lay.

was made from a presawn bundle of obechi, a wood that has little grain but slight variations of colour, which shows that it is an individually-laid deck.

The use of a flat steel rule is a good idea, but most of the difficulties of keeping thin strips of wood in discipline has to do with the application of glue, which can vary in thickness from the applicator. This arises because of the physical difficulty of applying glue to thin strips of flexible timber. A way of keeping the plank steady as the glue goes down is to place it in a sawn slot, as with the caulking jig. However the job is tackled, laying planks remains a very disciplined process, but constantly admired if it is well done – and more so than any other feature of the vessel.

The Forward Casemate and Boat Deck

In order to finish the planking, the walls of the superstructure had to be positioned, and piercings for the 4in gun ports for the casemate made. Aft the casemate walls is the boat deck, surrounded by blast screens designed to deflect shell and shot away from these vital and vulnerable small vessels. The gun port apertures of the casemate have to be carefully made, as they also acted in full scale as protection for the gun crew. In the early days of the ship's life, they were opened and closed as the gun traversed through its arc, and this detail of lowering the ports down onto the deck is included on the model, with working hinges.

The walls were made with 1/16in three-ply, clad with pewter sheet suitably riveted. At the same time, the aft funnel breastpiece fitted to the bulwark at the break of the ship was made and fitted. This cross member, into which the aft funnel fits, will eventually support two stump masts used for coaling duties.

▲ The first five planks laid on the fo'c'sle deck. The white dots in the waterway correspond with frame numbers on the subdeck, beneath the planking. It is important not to lose these reference points.

Looking now at the crescent-shaped section of B-turret's barbette, this armoured wall was made for the model using plywood, cut on the short grain and gently steamed into position. From the picture it is now possible to see very clearly the concept of the defence of both the ship and the space occupied by the boats. This is fortress mentality, protecting a vital portion of the ship in an armed citadel, and this concept will be repeated in the aft superstructure, which bristles with defensive guns.

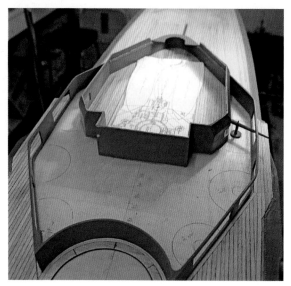

▲ Forward superstructure of the casemate, looking aft. The arc of travel for the 4in guns has been drawn on the deck and a dummy gun made to test the arc of fire, seen at the top right-hand side.

▲ Detail of the small sanding block at B-turret. The decking has been flooded with aliphatic glue to seal all the plank joints. This glue soaks away, and the total surface can then be finished to a satin shine, preferably sprayed on.

Fabricating Funnels

When viewed at a glance in profile, this ship may appear to have a single, flat-sided funnel. The smaller fore funnel is largely obscured by the tripod mast which dominates the superstructure. On more careful observation, the fore funnel can be seen clearly enough, but it was rightly criticised at the time of the launch as being wrongly sited, repeating a serious fault of the original *Dreadnought* (1905) design, about which there will be further discussion when it comes to the details of the tripod mast and gun-director's tower.

Funnels are highly significant shapes on ships, giving them in profile the definitive character of their class. They also carry a great deal of detail which it is not so easy to imitate at this scale. The nature of funnels in full size is that they are fabricated items made from sheet steel. In miniature, any attempt to make them of other material will affect how they appear as finished items. On the model, brass sheet was chosen for its strength and ductility, in the knowledge that it would have to be clad with pewter sheet for greater definition of riveting.

The Funnel Patterns

These were formed by soaking and steaming three-ply timber with a blowlamp acting on a length of copper tube, held in the engineer's vice. Only a low flame is required to persuade dampened timber into the round, aided by clamps which will bring plywood to the shape required. This looks difficult, if not nigh impossible, but the plain facts are that timber does not mind this process, and it strengthens wood – it does not weaken it. Anyone who has been involved with the making of violins, guitars, or any musical instrument which has curves, will bear testimony to the technique.

Soak the timber or plyboard well beforehand and gently wrap the timber round the heated tube. At first it will appear not to move very much, but then it starts to plasticise, in the proper sense of that word. Do not force it; let the wood take its own time. As the timber dries out along the length of the copper tube, dip it all in a bucket of water again. Watch out, however, when passing over the end of the tube – the exhaust gases will burn you with the heat expelled at the open end.

These funnel patterns are made simply to wrap the brass sheet around the funnel shape, and the reverse profile can be used for the other half, so there is no need to make more than one half for each funnel.

▲ Funnel pattern being formed in 1/16in birch three-ply.

▲ Demonstration of wrapping the brass around the half-pattern of the funnel.

▲ The half-funnel patterns placed in the casemate.

Annealing the Brass Sheet

The brass sheet must then be softened with heat to remove the natural spring of the material. The blowtorch needs to be quite fierce for this procedure, softening the metal so that it will take its shape from the former by being smoothed with hand pressure only, and jointed at the seam. Towards the end of the process, the funnel bandings are put on; they are kebab sticks planed in half, and steamed round, followed by more riveted pewter sheet. The funnel bases have cravats which act as collars on top of the airspace at the foot of the funnel. In full size, without these heat sinks the decks would have been scorched, so the air spaces play an important role at the base of all funnel systems. Two more cravats are fitted just beneath the funnel cages at the top banding, sloping out like the brim of a hat.

▲ The brass sheet being softened with the propane torch using a fierce flame.

▼ Aft funnel cage under construction using brass tube and wire.

The Funnel Cages

The funnel cages provided a means of covering the considerable areas of the open funnel tops with canvas when the boilers were down, and this prevented rainwater and damp air entering the flues, making fires even more difficult to raise for the stokers and trimmers. The cages also provided a grab rail for carrying out this work and any other maintenance issues on the interior of the funnels, which were fitted, in full scale, with a series of internal rung ladders. On the model, these cages were made with 1/16in brass tube for the outer rim, and with brass wire to the ridge, soft-soldered using an open flame technique.

This is a good moment to point out the difference between soldering a joint with a soldering iron, and sweating a joint, where the whole surface is heated to accept the solder flow. The latter process is preferable, if at all possible, because the metal expands to absorb the solder and it makes a much better joint as a result.

▲ An overlay of pewter sheet on the fore funnel. Note the half bandings made from barbecue sticks steamed round, and the cravat at the base of the funnel. Also in the picture is a close-up of the riveting wheel with engineer's slitting saw on the end of the handle.

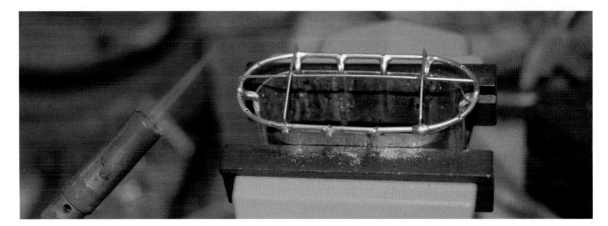

CHAPTER 4
∼*Armaments and Electronics* ∼

Protecting the Great Guns

Gun Turrets

Producing five identical gun turrets means turning to the principle of moulding in glass-reinforced polyester (GRP). This process begins with making a master pattern from a material which is stable, and relatively easy to carve. My preference for English lime comes about because it is cheap and available, but this work could be done in any timber which is close-grained and dimensionally stable. The turret shape was bandsawn out of the solid block of wood into its basic shape, and the sloping sides were cut by tipping the saw table to the appropriate angle. This job is ideally done in one sweep, but backed away from the true cut line, so it can then be hand-finished.

The round-faced spokeshave has been mentioned before as a tool which can put a concave shape into wood, leaving a smooth cut in its wake, but before doing this the carved piece must be attached firmly to a baseboard, using double-sided tape or retaining screws from the underside, otherwise the tool blade is likely to chatter. The spokeshave can then provide the subtle scalloped shape on the forward profile of the gun-housing.

In full size, the turret is designed to deflect shot and shell away from piercing through the armour-plated walls, from whichever angle the offensive shot is fired. This echoes the blast walls which protect the boat deck, and also in full scale a hidden internal deck called the protective deck, which is designed to deflect torpedoes and shell shot away from vital machinery just below the waterline. These spaces created in the wings of the ship's hull allowed coal to lie against the inside of the armoured plates, thus providing yet another barrier against the effects of penetration.

All these measures were worked into the dreadnought design, and made injury to these vessels relatively difficult to inflict compared to older designs. The three quite separate slopes on the roof of each turret were extra-thick armour-plate: this is emphasised on the model by using a different pitch of rivets – even bolder than those on the hull. The details of the three

gun-aiming hoods are the last items to be applied, before all the pewter sheet is overlaid ready for the moulding process.

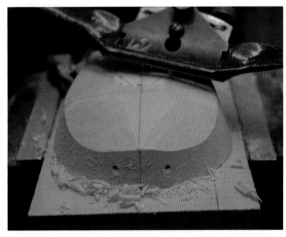

▲ Carving the gun turret pattern.

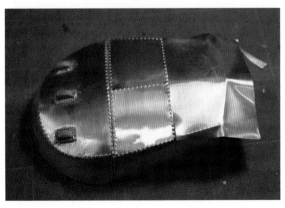

▲ Overlay of pewter sheet depicting armour plating.

The Silicone Rubber Mould for the Gun Turrets: The Lay-up

A box to contain the first pouring of silicone rubber is constructed: this must have sufficient depth and surrounding support for the mould to be stable when it is removed for use. This box needs to be constructed with a view to being able to deconstruct it later, so that the rubber mould may be released from it. It must also be well enough constructed to retain the grey rubber solution to be poured into it without the mixture leaking out.

The rubber compound is expensive, but this is no time to be saving on the amount to fill the total reservoir, which needs to be calculated in advance; do not mix too little because, under these circumstances, it is better to have a small surplus than suddenly to run short. Plasticine, or something similar, can be used to seal the mould box.

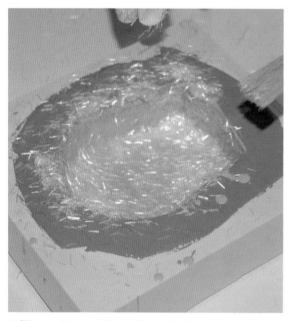
▲ Silicone rubber mould out of its retaining box.

▲ Ribbed roller for expelling air pockets.

The Cut-Line

The pattern is placed face down, with a spacer piece to increase slightly the depth of the moulding, as well as to provide a good trim line on the final edge. This spacer piece is made and cut out to match the bottom profile of the turret in 6mm MDF board, and the spacer piece sealed with any compound which will reject the solution sticking to it. In other words, it can be spray-painted or varnished. This one was sealed with shellac. After mixing up the rubber solution with the catalyst, the rubber mould is then sprayed with release agent and placed centrally. The detail on the pattern is stippled with a brush in order to make sure all the air is excluded, before the total mixture is poured all over the pattern. Pour the mixture from a height if possible (12cm or so), like a waiter pouring coffee. This stretches out the mix and it should land in a ribbon configuration and spread out naturally. It is then left to de-gas and cure off. When the mixture has fully cured, the box is dismantled, and the rubber mould can be released ready for the moulding process.

▲ Moulding of gun turret. Note the trim line.

The Moulding from the Mould

The resin gelcoat is then prepared and mixed with an additive to make it thixotropic. This resin mix is the outer layer of polyester, which makes direct contact with the detail of the rubber mould, and has to be well mixed with the curing agent according to the instructions on the tin.

A basic pattern of the shape to be moulded needs to be cut from the chopped mat strand (600g). For this turret shape, all that was needed was a roundish profile

▲ Sanded to the trim line.

▲ Removing the brim.

▲ Five turrets, first spray coat.

which would leave sufficient material at the top of the rubber mould to allow for shrinkage, and for a good trim line. The chopped mat strand needs to be 'worked', in order to take the stiffness out of the material, before it is laid down. This is done between the thumbs, suitably gloved, bending it and stretching it, until it is pliable enough to be pushed down into the mould. The chopped mat strand is then stippled in with a brush, which is properly called 'wetting out', and 'knocked down' with a small ribbed roller, which

eliminates any air between the mould and the lay-up. The excess resin is mopped up with a second brush kept handy for the purpose.

Finally, the rim excess is removed after it has all cured off and dried out. It becomes clear why a trim line (provided in this case by the 6mm flat piece inserted into the rubber pattern), which is part of the total mould on the inside, is a very desirable feature. This is common practice with GRP moulding, because the outer edge of any item which has been layered in GRP is always uneven in thickness and inclined to fracture. I am greatly indebted to Steve Taylor, who is a professional laminator of GRP, and whose gloved hands are in the accompanying photograph. This is a full mask operation, and the professional also wears rubber gloves to ward off the evil spirits.

The five identical turrets were sprayed with the grey bumper paint, and preparations put in place for the manufacture of the 13½in guns to be housed inside them.

The Great Guns

The 13½in gun was first fitted experimentally to the Majestic Class of Battleship in 1895. The barrels weighed 67 tons each, but were abandoned in favour of a new 12in barrel, with 113 miles of wire wound round the gun barrel between A and B tubes, right up to the chase. Every 8.4 miles of wire weighed a ton, and each gun took about nine months to manufacture, which had a most important bearing on the time required to build a battleship.

The Thames Iron Works had had a very long association with the shipbuilders and gunmakers of W G Armstrong (Newcastle) at Elswick. They had supplied the original guns fitted to their first battleship HMS *Warrior* in 1860: the infamous rifle breech-loading 110pdrs, which were used individually as bow and stern chasers. A further eight of them were sited on the gun deck below, flanking the twenty-six traditional muzzle-loading 68pdrs. The 110pdr RBLs were so dangerous for the gun crews to operate that they were withdrawn from service by 1863. The problem lay with the vent piece, which had a propensity to be forced explosively out of the breech, because of a lack of the correct material to make a gasket which would be repeatedly gas-tight. The rings were made of copper and they quickly distorted.

Given that HMS *Monarch*, one of the four Orion Class battleships ordered, was being built at Elswick at the same time as *Thunderer* was being constructed on the Thames, it is a reasonable assumption that Armstrong Whitworths would have received the order to make the forty barrels required for all four ships. This beautiful theory was brought to a swift end when I read a recently-posted article by Steve Woodward on www.shipsnostalgia.com. In this highly-detailed account of the ship's life, he states that the Orion Class guns were constructed by Vickers, built in their Barrow-in-Furness workshops, and designated the MkV L. I was delighted to read in the same paragraph that these guns were so well made that they survived to defend the Straits of Dover during World War II. It is an excellent technical article, which I would re-commend for further reading. The new gun came with high performance claims, firing a shell weighing 1250lb from a 45-calibre gun. The claim was that this projectile would have greater smashing power, and would inflict more damage after penetrating armour plating, than any gun so far tested. At the same time, it employed less muzzle velocity because of the increased size of bore, and for this reason the gun barrel would have a longer life. The total weight of shot which the ship could deliver was calculated to be 12,500lb against the 6,800lb of her namesake *Dreadnought*. I take it from these claims that the word super-dreadnought means in terms of firepower alone that the Orion Class

battleship had almost twice the capacity of the original dreadnoughts launched only seven years previously. Dimensionally speaking, *Thunderer* was only 55ft greater in length than *Dreadnought*, so that it represented big progress in terms of the all-on-the-centreline big gun ship.

Gravity Casting

Manufacture in Miniature

These gun barrels were made in miniature by turning a pattern from brass bar, setting the top-slide on the lathe over at a very fine angle to taper the barrel slowly to the correct profile as detailed on the plan. As well as the taper, towards the mouth of the barrel there is a small swelling at the muzzle, so the narrowest section is approximately seven-eighths down the barrel. The barrel was also bored out at this point, and the detail of the barrel lining included at the muzzle. This appears as an annular ring.

As with the turrets, this pattern was destined to produce ten identical barrels including the trunnions, which are the short lengths of bar on which the barrels

▼ Master pattern for the 13½in gun.

pivot, and by which they are supported. This involves cross-drilling the barrel, which is best done by boring a hole from either side. Small drills wander off course, given the slightest chance, so this is the only safe way of proceeding.

Silicone Mould for the 13½in Guns

RTV101 is a silicone rubber mix that has been developed to resist temperatures of up to approximately 400°C, which means that it can be used with low-melt metals for metal casting. This has great significance and application for scratch builders, who can now make their own castings, and it is done in the following manner.

A mould wall is constructed out of any material which will not allow silicone to adhere to it. In this case I am using Lego bricks, which allow for different shapes and sizes of mould pattern boxes, and for assembly and disassembly, and the standard size of Lego bricks are ideally suited for the purpose. At the bottom of the mould box, cut a piece of Plastikard or similar to act as a base, or there will be a dimply bottom to the mould.

The pattern, in this case the gun barrel, is first sprayed with release agent, and then lowered into a mix of dental plaster, to the halfway point of the pattern. It may need a little pressure to press it down, but do this swiftly, as the plaster sets very quickly. I refer to the mix as dental plaster: the proprietary name is Herculite, but other similar products will be stocked by glassfibre merchants.

Mark out the location pins, by using a handheld twist drill, but only go down 2cm or so. This will mean that when the two halves come together, they will exactly locate the top half of the mould to the bottom half. Where the location pins are put does not greatly matter. This mould has six of them.

Pour in the mixture over the top of the dental plaster and all over the pattern. It takes twelve hours or so to cure. When the rubber has hardened, it may be separated from the dental plaster, and then placed in the bottom half of the mould.

With the barrel back in place, the walls of the mould need to be built up for the second half. Another coat of release agent is sprayed onto the inside of the mould, and more solution mixed and poured, filling the mould to the brim. Allow another twelve hours to pass, and then separate the two halves. They should peel apart once the joint line has been found, and release the pattern.

▲ Gun barrel pattern suspended in plaster. The first pouring of rubber has taken place.

▲ Second pouring of rubber.

▲ Two halves of rubber mould clamped; metal poured into ingate.

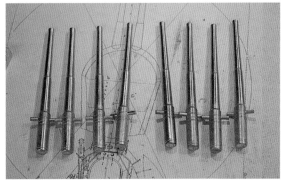

▲ Eight barrels cast.

An ingate or funnel needs to be cut into the top of the mould, so that the metal can be poured into the mould. On a simple pattern like this, cut out a cone shape with a sharp scalpel in the shape of a funnel, for ease of pouring.

Two supporting pieces of board, the same shape as the mould exterior, need to be cut to maintain the stability of the mould when it is clamped together, tightly enough not to allow the molten metal to escape, but not so tightly that it distorts the mould.

Talcum powder is used as a parting agent, and this should be dusted into the two halves of the mould, using a soft brush to smooth it all round the mould interior.

The dross is removed from the crucible, and when the metal is good and fluid, a steady pouring down the ingate completes the job. Put a tray underneath, just in case there is a problem or slight splashing.

The first two or three castings are never the best. This has to do with the hardening process of the rubber, but it is a good idea to do a batch at a time, because when the mould gets hot, the metal finds its way to the furthest extremities, and reproduces the detail with great definition.

The cheeks of the gun carriages, as well the turret floors, have to be constructed so that with the ten barrels, five removable floors, fifteen cheeks and five circular barbette bases, the main armament is ready for positioning. The turrets are set on the centre line and on station lettered in the usual way. A-turret is the one farthest forward; B-turret is the forward facing, super-firing turret above; Q-turret is amidships, followed by X as the aft super-firing turret; Y is the aftmost.

From the outset the turrets were always going to rotate but, as will be seen later, they do rather more than that. Centring them was an all-day task as they must be absolutely in line: if they are not, it would be very obvious.

With the large offensive guns safely on station, both the fore and aft superstructures are the next items for manufacture. It would, of course, be possible to have the guns fitted with elevation of the barrels, but the conclusion was that it was best to fix them, and the jig shows how they were kept at exactly the same angle. Anything else looks a trifle odd, but many warship photographs exist with barrels ranged at differing heights.

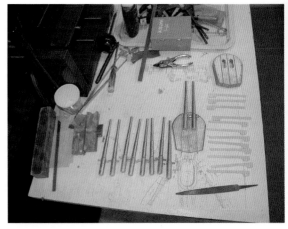

▲ Barrels set in cheeks on turret floor.

▲ Turret hood slides over the barrels.

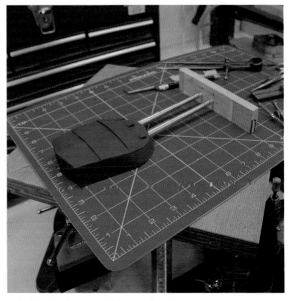

▲ Jig for the alignment of the gun barrels.

The Protection of the Ship

The Fore Conning Tower

This 12in armour-plated pillbox, placed on top of the navigation house, is the command position for the whole ship. In action, this is the place where the captain 'fought his ship', and where his orders would be carried out. To hand he had voice pipes, electric bells, indicators, telegraphs, and a chief quartermaster at the wheel and compass. From here he could give orders to the navigating officer, the gunnery officer and the torpedo officer, with direct contact to the gun barbettes, all gun positions and torpedo flats, ammunition passages and watertight door stations, signal stations and engine rooms, so that he could in a few seconds communicate with any part of the ship.

Placed just behind super-firing turret B, it also incorporated a siting tower for the forward gunnery, a rangefinder, and a simple form of gun-director with a firing key for each broadside. The strange kidney-shaped blob was a slab of extra armoured plate rounded off, which would have caught anything ricocheting off B-turret, and hopefully deflected it elsewhere. It is riveted up to show the detail of construction, but remains the least shipshape item I have ever been asked to replicate.

▲ Conning tower surmounting the navigation officer's cabin.

The Foredeck

There is yet more deck planking to be done on this raised platform, over the six 4in gun housings beneath, and two further 4in guns, which are to be mounted virtually unprotected, apart from a dwarf wall adjacent to turret B. The varnish being applied to the decks is satin shine, as a top coat after several applications of aliphatic glue, sanded down to a super-smooth finish.

▼ Construction of forward conning tower.

▲ Q-turret amidships.

▲ Aft superstructure with expanded aluminium mesh.

The Aft Bridge

The aft bridge on the upper deck is designed for the 4in guns to defend the ship, and also provides the raised platforms for searchlights and rangefinding. There are two concave walls to be fabricated, and four gun ports for the secondary armament on this lower level of the ship. Four more operate on the level above, plus four small signal guns.

On the model, 1/16in ply was once again used, and the curves steamed to form the sweep of Q-turret's barrels, and also the aft end of X-barbette. Eventually, this whole section will lift off, so the citadel is made to slot into the subdeck, with a margin board around the base.

The decks have been metalled with imitation treadplate, set in aliphatic resin glue, later to be sprayed. This is made from expanded aluminium mesh, flattened down. The original decks were covered with metal in order to avoid the likelihood of setting fire to the deck boards. The overhead view shows the positions of the decking which has yet to be added, which support the searchlight platform and aft gun-director. The bight out of the trailing edge is to prepare the way for the installation of the aft conning tower.

Buttresses

Building up the walls in full size required internal buttressing with triangular pieces whose weight had been reduced by cutting out their centres. When metal is treated in this fashion, it is referred to as having been 'lightened'. This detail comes from the Science Museum model of the sister ship *Monarch*, and does add realism, in the way that under certain light conditions it casts shadows which look very realistic.

▲ Buttress supports to the protective blast walls.

These little reinforcements are to be found all around the ship's walls wherever there is an upright and unsupported face.

Ladders

Courtesy and accommodation ladders come in different sizes and require different lengths and widths. The tread of the ladder must adopt the correct angle to match the desired incline, each step being horizontal with the deck. The challenge of building a twenty-seven-step ladder requires a jig to keep the angles constant and the veneer strips in place when they are being glued together. It is vital that ladders are made to look light, which is why at this scale they require the thinnest section of timber in the workshop. At 1:96 scale, the plank thickness is 0.5mm.

▲ Laddermaking jig. Note the projecting tooth spacer.

▲ Side one of ladder under construction on sawn jig.

▲ Accommodation ladder of twenty-seven steps.

The Ladder Jig

To cut regular slots with a machine saw, you need to make a simple jig with a detent spaced between the saw blade – in this case a bandsaw – at the distance required for each increment. The backing board is set at the desired angle for the tread, and has a thin piece of ply sticking out of it, like a tooth. This projection must match the width of the saw-blade cut, known as the kerf. At the beginning of the process, the first slot in the comb is cut freehand, and then fed into the tooth. When that one has been machined, the next one follows, maintaining an equal spacing throughout.

The sawn piece then becomes the jig for holding the ladder treads in place during assembly. The treads must be square-ended and cut to equal lengths, because the timber is too thin to make any receiving slot, and relies simply on the strength of a butt-joint and glue.

In order to avoid the ladder adhering to the jig, it will need to be waxed with polish, and the addition of electrician's plastic tape will stop any adhesion at the bottom of the holding jig. It is a good idea to varnish the veneer timber all over before any gluing takes place, so that the glue spots do not show. The first side of the ladder is the most difficult to fit, but using a spatula to line up all the treads on the backside, so that there is a gap between the toothed jig and the upright of the ladder, means that the treads will only stick to the ladder, and not to the jig. The upright of the ladder, properly called a stile, is glued with aliphatic resin along its whole length, on the inside face, and is clamped with hair clips. When dried, the glue does not show, provided that it has been previously sealed with varnish. When the glue has cured off, the other upright stile is relatively easy to attach with yet more hair clips, whose ends might have been customised for the work. These aluminium clips are excellent workhorses for all kinds of light clamping operations, but if I am going to buy some extras, I always take my wife with me, as they are sourced from ladies' hairdressers.

The different deck levels and platforms on *Thunderer* require a multiplicity of ladders, but the most handsome are the accommodation ladders fitted to the stern of the ship. They are also removable from this station when required elsewhere. They are detailed, when at sea, as hanging on the walls of the wash deck stowed behind the whalers. The colour of the varnished obechi wood with several layers of French polish makes a welcome contrast with the grey walls of the ship, and are a feature which emphasise the scale of this vessel and the height of the aft deck above the water.

Secondary Armament

Defence of the Ship: The 4in Guns (C50 MkVII)

Separate scale drawings for these weapons do not exist as far as I know, but there are some very helpful earlier versions of this gun drawn up by John Roberts in his book, as mentioned before. They are shown in plan view and in elevation on *Thunderer*'s building plans, so their vital statistics are well established. With items like this, it is as well to get them onto a drawing board, which also has the advantage for a constructor of thinking how they can best be modelled.

The decision was taken to make the patterns up in brass for centrifugal casting. There are three main components to be cast: the gun cradle, which includes the cheeks and slots for the trunnions; the circular pedestal gun-mounting, which has a sacrificial stub end to centre into the lathe for boring out the pivot; and lastly, the gun recoil cylinder mounted on top of the barrel. The other details of the training wheel, the elevating hand-wheel, and the range dial, were all additions to the main structure and were turned on the lathe.

Wheels could, of course, have been cast, but brass wheels make a good contrast with all the other matt grey, and it is permissible to leave them unpainted. In fact, it looks more realistic if they are left in their natural state. The two telescopic sights mounted on either side of the recoil piston can also be left as though polished. Eventually they will dull, but they will retain that distinctive look of an item which is in regular use aboard, polished by use. The completed model 4in gun has the ability to swivel, depress and elevate, and all the wheels go round.

According to Steve Woodward, the MkVII gun was designed to fire a 31lb shell to a range of 11,500 yards at a rate of approximately six rounds per minute.

Casting in a Centrifuge

The basic principles of casting in a centrifuge are no different from gravity casting, except that a single mould can be made for many components to be cast at once, which saves on time and money. The big advantage of a centrifuge is that, because the mould is spinning during the casting process, the liquid metal is forced into the furthest corners and the tiniest crevices, and long thin items become a possibility, as do other more complicated patterns.

The skill is in making the mould in the first place and, as with gravity-poured moulds, the first part of the operation involves suspending the pattern horizontally, not this time in dental plaster as mentioned under gravity casting, but using the more professional material called Chavant. This plasticine-like medium is gently warmed: an electric oven plate-warmer is ideal, so that patterns can be pressed halfway into the surface.

Because the final mould material (RTV, or Room Temperature Vulcanizing) is firm but flexible when cured, pressing down the pattern to the absolute halfway mark in the Chavant clay is not vital, but it is desirable to avoid undercut, or the release of a pattern may prove to be difficult. It is possible to trim around the Chavant with a scalpel after the pattern has been placed, and whilst the Chavant is still warm. A good technique is to press the patterns in slightly beyond their halfway point, and gently excavate to the joint line by eye, with a sculptor's scalpel or a small screwdriver blade.

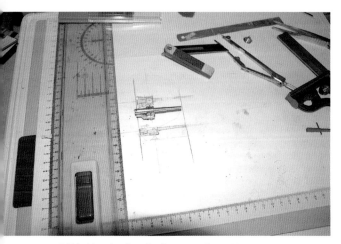

▲ Working drawings for 4in gun casting patterns.

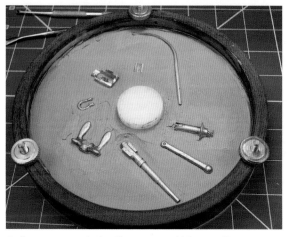

▲ 4in gun patterns in the Chavant material for centrifuge.

▲ First pouring of rubber solution over the Chavant.

▲ Both halves poured and separated.

The items to be cast need to be placed and arranged in the mould in such a way that the centrifugal force enters most easily. Surprisingly, this is in an anticlockwise direction. Items also need to be moderately balanced, or the machine will start to vibrate when the metal is cast.

There is an aluminium plate at the base of the mould underneath the Chavant material; in the centre is a removable nylon plug which is the bottom plug of the first half of the moulding process. Lastly, there is an outer ring, which has holes for the three studs and wheel nuts drilled through it, allowing for the joining of the bottom and top plates. These items all have to fit well, to avoid leakage at any point in the proceedings. The three location buttons are made at this point in the Chavant, with a round-headed stud pressed into the moulding material, so that when cast the top half of the mould will align perfectly with the bottom half. Parting agent is then sprayed over the patterns and the Chavant. Nothing after this process must touch the patterns, or fingerprints will show.

The RTV rubber is thoroughly mixed with the catalyst, and carefully poured over the pattern details, before the main pouring by hand to the lip of the ring. I do the former with a much smaller pot, making sure the rubber has flowed evenly over all of the details of the cast objects. I then make the major pouring from a larger pot, filling the mould up to the level of the outer ring. With the centrifuge running, the final topping to the first half of the mould is done with the addition of the hollow nylon plug sealing the whole (first half) mould in an airtight fashion. When the rubber solution in the mould has cured (I leave it for at least twelve hours), it is separated from the Chavant clay using nylon jacking screws, supplied with the centrifuge,

which force the mould ring off the bottom plate.

On reassembly, the first half of the moulding has the patterns replaced into it (some patterns stick to the rubber and some to the Chavant) and a thorough coat of release agent sprayed over it. A differently-shaped nylon centre plug ring is added, which will provide a chamber for receiving the molten metal through the top aluminium plate. This plug is known as the reservoir plug, and eventually from it all the sprue lines will be cut to allow the metal to run to the objects being cast. The top ring, or wall of the mould, is added and clamped down with longer studs on the outer edge, to allow for the extra height needed for the second pouring of rubber.

Before the machine is set to run, the patterns once again have to be covered carefully with the smaller pot of rubber, and then flooded by hand, with the larger catalysed mix, to the brim of the outer wall. The top

▲ First cast: note that the radial davit has not worked because it requires ventilation via a 1mm hole.

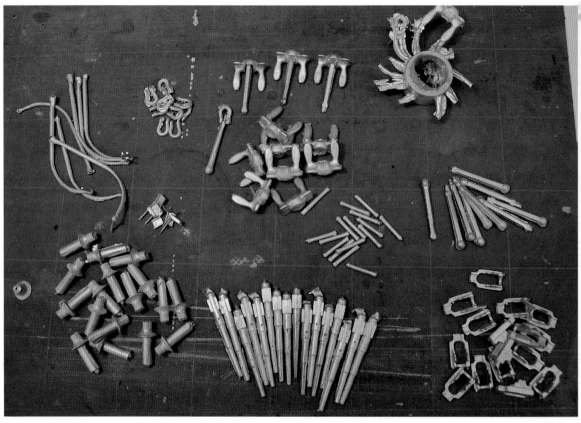

▲ Subsequent castings improve.

▼ Sixteen 4in guns detailed with telescopic sights and adjusting wheels.

plate is then added, the centrifuge set to run, and the last hollows topped up with the smaller plastic cup, until the rubber starts to overflow. This done, a nylon guide ring, and a topping-out plug with a hollow centre, are pushed into the top plate until the solution feeds and overflows from the spout, and no air is left in the chamber.

The resulting second pouring has to be left until the rubber has hardened off. This process happens from the outer face first, so that the inner surface may still be soft. Follow the advice given in the handbook, and do not be tempted to open the mould simply because it has hardened off on the outside.

The parting agent allows for separation, and the two halves can then be split open. Once again, both halves are best left for a few hours to harden off. The sprue lines, in which the molten metal runs from the central reservoir to the pattern, can now be cut. Lino-cutting tools are recommended for this, but I use a 2mm spoon gouge, which does the job just as well.

The sprue runs have to be cut in sympathy with the

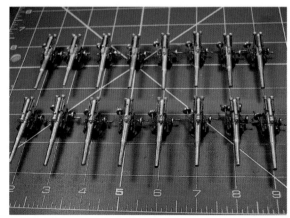

anticlockwise motion of the centrifuge. There will be no trouble with the larger square items, but the long thin shapes, characterised by the radial davit seen in the picture, may need a small breather hole drilled through the rubber at the extreme end, to allow the metal to vent. Sprue runs can be made top and bottom, but in practice this seems to be unnecessary.

The Melt Pot

The matching piece of kit for the centrifuge is admittedly a luxury, because you could heat the metal up in a ladle, using an open flame as in gravity casting, and probably get away with it. There is, however, a close relationship between the running speed of the centrifuge, and the temperature of the metal being poured, according to how each particular mould performs, and each mould is slightly different. This means having to experiment initially, which is no bad thing, because it hardens off the rubber mould with each pouring, giving better definition, and the metal can simply be returned into the pot, so no extra expense is involved.

Talcum powder, dusted into the mould with a very soft brush, helps the metal to run much more easily. If the metal will not reach the furthest point of the mould, then a small 1mm drill is used at the end of the pattern, and the hole goes through the rubber mould. This is normally enough to allow the pattern to be completed, but it will mean that when the patterns are removed, the tiny sprue piece needs to be removed carefully, or it will tear the rubber mould.

If the mould does not work very well at first, continue to experiment with improving the sprue lines, but be aware that all moulds improve with use, and skills are quickly learned with practical experience.

The mould may be used indefinitely, as RTV does not decay. I have perfectly usable gravity moulds which are over twenty-five years old, with no apparent deterioration.

The Molten Metal

The metal used was a proprietary metal known as K2 – other such metals are available. It arrives in ingot form, and becomes molten at around 350°C. When cast, it is just hard enough to cut a thread with a die. You can also machine it in a lathe, which is important for many truing-up operations, like the manufacture of wheels or the need to cross-drill or bore out. You can solder to it with ultra-low-temperature solder, providing there is sufficient thickness of material, and it is receptive to being glued with the many adhesives these days advertised as adhering to metal. If drilling this metal with a fine drill, use Renaissance wax as a lubricant. This microcrystalline wax will not allow the bit to clog or snatch. I keep it constantly by my side.

The real plus factor is that there is no limitation put on the modeller by having to fabricate each item appearing on the ship's plans, and with model shipbuilding there are real benefits and bonuses to be had by using a centrifuge. Artistically speaking, castings have a particular look all their own, which transfers into miniature – something to do with having minutely rounded edges; whatever it is, the human eye can detect it.

The Hawse Collars

The last production task in my old workshop in December 2006 was to make a wooden pattern of the hawse collars and gravity-cast three of them. Their unique shape is entirely functional, and in full scale protected the deck planking from injury, caused by the massive studded links of the bower anchor chains on either side of the ship. The sheet anchor, on the starboard side only, was placed there for emergency use.

The shanks of the stockless anchors were hove up with shackles attached to the anchor ring, all housed in

▲ Deck hawse piercings.

▲ Lady's fingernails plus cast deck hawse collars and grilles.

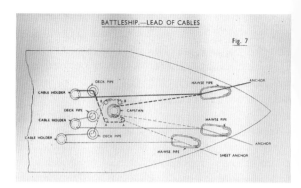

▲ Battleship lead of cables illustration. Source: *Manual of Seamanship 1937.*

the chute. This relatively large opening has a detachable grille over it as a safety feature; in real life, it would be heavily greased, and therefore easy for a seaman to lose his footing with dire consequence and, very possibly, fatal injury.

On the model it would be almost a year before the metal collars were fitted in December 2007, following the considerable upheaval of moving a workshop which had been in place for over twenty-four years, and designing and fitting out a new one.

Cutting Through the Deck

Assaulting the structure of the decking in this delicate area of the ship is one of those jobs best done first thing in the morning. The issue at stake at here is to do with the alignment of the chute outlet and the centre point of the hawse collar. It is all perilously close to the outer edge of the gunwale. The chute inclines at a steep angle, so the best way of going about this task is first to drill a small hole at right angles through a carefully-measured pattern on the deck. Masking tape is not only good for marking out, it also prevents drill bits from creeping or running away. The same technique is required here as was used for boring out the propeller shafts. The operator must go in vertically with a small centre drill, and then use larger drills for boring out the angle. The use of a needle file is also a good idea for checking the angle of entry. What I would not recommend is simply cutting out the hawse holes in one go. For them to look as they should, the sloping relief angle on the backside of the cut must be visible, because light will fall on it in a special way. If the slopes do not look like ladies' fingernails, then a trick has been missed.

Electronics

A Static Working Model

Quite late on in the proceedings the conclusion was that it would be a good idea to have the turrets revolve, which these days is quite possible to put into effect with proportional radio control. What may seem like an innocent request has far-reaching consequences. Cutting five housings in the barbettes for the servo motors, making a removable box to house the radio-control (R/C) receiver under the boat deck, and cutting through the deck lying beneath the aft superstructure, were all things which were possible, but meant a great deal of careful measuring and planning. The issue most on my mind was how to devise a method of retaining the central pivots of the R/C servos in line. Any deviation from dead centre would show, but in order to have the servo housing cut out, those centres would have physically to disappear.

▲ Deck hatch being cut for radio-control receiver.

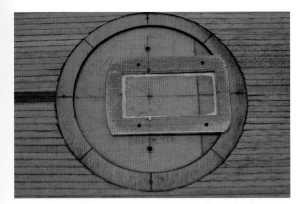

▲ Pattern for the exact positioning of servo on centre line of ship.

Methods of Attack

The finest saw-cut available to the modeller is the razor saw, but attacking a finished deck has to be done with the utmost care and forward planning. A metal edge-guide is a good way to start a saw kerf, by supporting the edge of a blade at 90 degrees. Make an initial cut first with a razor knife-blade or scalpel; this will allow the teeth of the razor saw to run in the small groove which a scalpel cut makes. A saw of any kind will always follow the line of least resistance. Because there is going to be side pressure on the metal guide, it is best screwed into position, and the saw-cut begun in the centre. Another tip is to tape up the teeth on the back of the saw, so that it is prevented from accidentally cutting through any object at the back of the blade. Further to all this, if you wish to disguise a hatchway, the best way to do it is to zigzag the planks; this involves chiselling out every alternate plank on the hatchway, and doing the same on the deck, giving a comb effect which the eye has a difficulty in following. Whereas this will disguise the opening, if there is to be regular use of the hatch, as is the case here, it is better just to have a straightforward hatch. A saw with a back support to it, like a tenon saw, will not cut successfully to the last part of the 90 degree corner, so that has to be knifed out: neither pleasant nor easy, and actually quite dangerous with an open blade. As always – go gently.

Siting the Servos

The servo chambers, under the gun barbettes, were tackled with a metal hacksaw blade holder, after very carefully marking the intercepts of the centre point, where the servo drive cogwheel must lie at dead centre because the whole gun turret has to pivot from this point.

The Radio-Control Receiver Box

To make a successful wooden box which is removable is no easy matter. This box has to fit through the aperture, with all its wiring in place. It must also allow for being drawn up on the underside of the deck with bolts, and requires careful alignment of bolts to nuts. The fitting of a crossbar to hold it into position as the bolts are tightened is also an essential. It will need a wide flange on which to set the bolts, but not interfere with posting it down the hole. The component parts to be fitted are the on/off switch for the receiver, the receiver itself, and also a rechargeable battery pack lying beneath, in a separate compartment. Cut into the sides of the box are the wiring slots on three sides, including a wide slot for the aerial fingers, which are made from a stiff wire, and must be separated in order to receive signal commands from the transmitter.

▲ The receiver box and battery housing.

Wiring

It is a bad idea to have wiring which is so tight that it is not possible to remove the receiver box easily. If in doubt, always add extension pieces to the wiring length, available as proprietary items, so that the box is not difficult to handle. Because proportional radio control is all magic to me, I will explain the particular set-up with this model. The wiring is arranged so that A- and B-turrets are synchronised, as are X and Y. Amidships, Q-turret is independent. This is done by using a Y-coupling for the fore and aft turrets, and a single line feeding into one of the six channels available on the small receiver box. The bottom channel in the receiver is the power line, fed by the rechargeable battery pack beneath. There is also a feed line for the charger to recharge the battery pack. An input socket is disguised on the port side wash deck bulwark. The effect of this circuitry is that all the guns may be made to train onto a target and, with practice, all may be made to move together. The only limiting factor is that the total sweep of a standard servo is approximately 60 degrees. There are servos manufactured, called retracts, which are used on model aircraft for activating the undercarriage. These have a full 180-degree sweep, but they do not self-centre again, which is a requirement for gun turrets. Transmitters these days have a refinement for adjusting the centring of the servo, so that in practical terms the gun barrels can be exactly aligned, and will return to their station when the proportional joystick on the transmitter is returned to centre.

Whereas all this is happening under the boat deck on the model, in full-size practice it is the conning tower to which all the communication systems were wired and piped as the nerve centre of the ship. There must have been an endless profusion of trunking to that relatively small turret, a nightmare to sort out when things went wrong. Later on I will discuss the lighting of the ship through a separate 12v DC system. The radio-control receiver works on a 4.7v DC system with a battery pack rated at 1300 milliamps. This is heavier duty than standard, with the result that it takes longer

to charge up. The transmitter and the receiver both have a single and dedicated transformer, so that there is no need to be concerned about inappropriate voltages when recharging the batteries.

Speaking as one whose only way to control a model in his childhood was to tie a piece of string to it, I remain astounded at the now commonplace ability to control objects remotely, with such precision, and in my case, with very limited knowledge of what is actually happening.

▲ Aft turrets X and Y wired together for synchronised creep.

▼ Radio-control installation.

CHAPTER 5

Masts

The Tripod and Upper Platforms

The Tripod Mast

The distinctive and innovative feature common to all British dreadnought battleships is the tripod mast. The departure from the need to have a masting system, which required neither forestays nor backstays nor other guyed support, meant that these ships were finally freed from the limitations imposed by ropes and wires on their arcs of fire, which had been the bugbear of battleships in the pre-dreadnought era. Certainly, there were stays supporting the funnels, and such items as canvas awning lines and blast screens, but nothing to stop the ship from being prepared quickly for action stations or general quarters.

The new three-legged mast also had several other desirable features in that it provided, in the case of the

Orion Class, support for the fore funnel, and also the raised platforms for the wheelhouse and the admiral's chart house. Above that is sited the manoeuvring compass platform, with its extended walkway running out above the conning tower. The flying triangular projection which supports the aft side of the fore funnel is known as the canopy, but its true mechanical role is to give firm support to the splay of the tubular legs. In full size both the forelegs and the mainmast have internal ladders to give access to the gun direction and fire control positions, and a certain protection for those who have duties aloft.

When I first studied the model of HMS *Monarch* (1911), sister ship of *Thunderer*, in the London Science Museum, I looked at the complications of installing all these platforms within the captive crescendo of an expanding tripod, and knew that it presented the most difficult fitting job on the whole vessel. There are two possibilities for the modelmaker faced with a sliding, bevel angle. The first is to make all the items of decking before assembling the work, mount the poles through the deck and then slide them on one by one, and somehow solder the joint at the top. The second possibility, and the one which I chose, is to start by silver-soldering the joint of the three poles at the head of the mast, and cutting slots which permit the decks to be slid from the base of the mast into their correct location. This arrangement also applies to the slots at the base of the mast, but they are easy enough to mask with the astragals which were a feature on the prototype.

▲ Silver-soldering the forelegs to the upright mainmast.

◀ The tripod mast and attendant platforms.

69

The Forelegs and Mainmast

As with so many other items of assembly, a jig is required for the interim stage. A full-sized, short wooden plank, with two blocks on the underside at either end to raise the plank off the bench, allows by experiment for finding the correct angle of splay to the forelegs and mainmast (8.5 degrees). The mainmast is absolutely vertical to the ship's keel. Silver-soldering is preceded by filing a half-round groove into the side of each foreleg, in order to make a snug joint with the upright mainmast. The three legs are then wired together, prepared with the Easiflo 2 flux, and silver-soldered with the large-nozzled propane torch. Soldering brass tube is easier than soldering solid bar, but both caution and courage are required, because the tube wall is very thin. The best technique is to reach the melting temperature of silver solder as quickly as possible. Failure to do this will burn out the flux, and not long after that, the flame will start to melt the brass, which is only 1/32in thick. The tubing is a K&S Metals product, which being American in origin, is still measured in imperial: forelegs 13/32in and mainmast 15/32in.

▲ Brace and bit for the mainmast seating.

On 22 January 2008 at 5.57pm, Lady Luck was with me: she is not always present. The soldered joint was successfully made, but no further work was done that day. Two days later, in order to seat the newly-made mast, the boat deck was assaulted with a full-sized shipwright's brace and bit, so that the tripod could take its rightful place amidships. This old-fashioned tool, because of its length, will give a much more accurate result than a fancy electric drill if you have to make a vertical piercing, but a good result does depend on having a sharp auger bit to accompany it, or it will tear the end-grain out of the miniature deck planks.

The Fore Bridge Platform Deck

As a core material, 1/16in birch ply is used for the two upper platforms surrounding the fore funnel. Planking on both sides avoids a tendency to warp on unsupported edges, although one can never guarantee that timber will not develop a mind of its own. I use mahogany for the edges, the correct name for which is the cants. This is laid on its edge and the grain of this hardwood helps to stabilise any tendency to warp, as well as giving a pleasing finish. Where the curves of the edging demand tight curvature, soaking and steaming the timber is employed, using the hot copper tube techniques described earlier.

▲ Underside of fore bridge platform.

The Admiral's Deck and Manoeuvring Compass Platform

This was made in the same style as the platform below, but not following exactly the 1911 lines, because at some stage in the ship's development the manoeuvring compass platform was extended, matching her sister

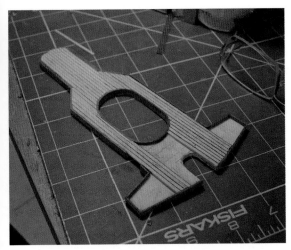

▲ Manoeuvring compass platform being planked.

▲ Platforms which surround the fore funnel.

ship HMS *Monarch*. The original plans show that the platform did not fully encircle the fore funnel, which would have made communications between the admiral's chart house and those working on the compass platform much more tiresome.

The Admiral's Chart House and the Wheelhouse
In amongst all the drab grey metal of this ship, comes a throwback to timber for the admiral's chart house, and at the fore end of this flying deck, the wheelhouse: glowing mahogany, at least in model form, which harks back to Edwardian domestic furnishing. Cabinetmakers and craftsmen at the height of the British Empire had their hands on the finest timbers available from all over the globe, and took great delight in showing their sundry skills whenever possible. Their distinctive trademark was in panelling, using moulding planes to

▲ Admiral's chart house and wheelhouse housed between the platform decks.

beautify every nook and cranny with complicated hidden joints, before the days of plywood and resin glues. Internally, these battleships were lavishly fitted out by modern standards, particularly in the quarters of the higher ranks.

The only way the modeller can imitate these extravagancies is to use veneer as an overlaid timber. Veneer is still obtainable in great variety, and was used on the model for both the wheelhouse and the chart house. The panelled door of the chart house is left ajar, and brass window frames contrast with the dark honey-colour of mahogany, which has several coats of French garnet polish to give it age and *gravitas*. This finish would not be suitable for a working model, because spirit varnish is not waterproof, but similar oil-based varnishes could be substituted easily. There is, however, something unique about the glow of French polish.

The Ship's Wheel
I do like a ten-spoked wheel. Whether or not the Orion Class battleships were fitted with eight-, ten- or twelve-spoked wheels, I cannot say; all I have to go on is the dimensions taken from the elevation plan. Making an item of this nature look right is not easy. Most of the proprietary wheels I see look a little lumpy. The trick is to under-scale the item where possible, and with a really small object, it is always easier to make it from metal. The central boss is the key item to watch with all wheel-wrighting, and if you are lucky enough to possess a lathe with some form of indexation from the bull wheel to divide the circle into the desired angles, then wheel making is not too difficult. Even easier, but more expensive, is a free-standing indexer, with a division plate, which I originally bought with the propeller manufacture in mind, or at least that is my excuse.

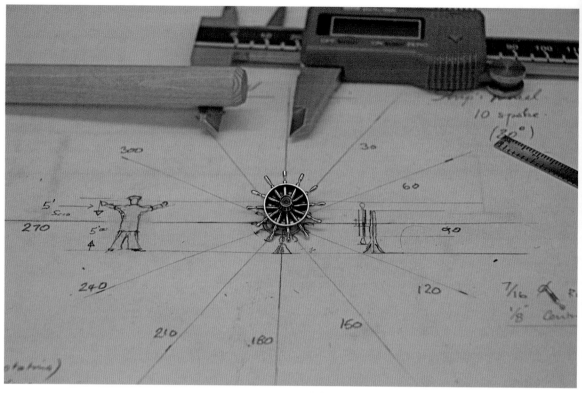

▲ Working drawings for ten-spoked wheel.

The Boss and Rim Technique

This is a useful way of overcoming the matching of spokes from the boss to the outer rim, and it will work at any scale. A solid bar of brass is first bored out with a D-bit set in the tool holder, leaving a central hub in the brass bar. The groove made by the D-bit is taken out to the rim, and deep-bored with sufficient depth to allow for both the depth of the rim and also for parting-off at the end of the process. The solid bar is then transferred to the indexer, and the divisions marked out with a centre drill. A sized drill is then used to break through the outer rim and also locate through to the boss. Only pierce the boss – do not drill through it; it is only to locate the spoke in this sort of scale. This will give a perfect match from the rim to the centre of the hub, which is a difficult thing to do otherwise. The whole item can then either be silver-soldered, or more realistically, soft-soldered. Silver-soldering is always preferable, but at this scale, and with the item still joined to the solid bar, you will most likely melt the brass spokes before the solder starts to flow. Once soldered, the solid brass bar can be put back into the lathe chuck, a central spindle bored through and then parted off, leaving a perfectly-made wheel. The spokes, and any other small-handled item like oar handles, are most easily made using the technique of a small electric drill, rotating against a moving abrasive strap – so both machines are running together. This takes a little practice, but produces a handle which is truly rounded and to scale.

▲ Wheel hub of ship's wheel.

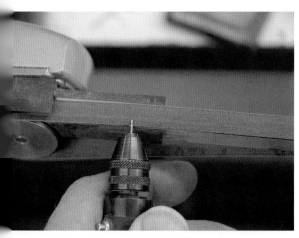

▲ Revolving abrasive strap and electric drill both in motion to make small handle.

▲ Ship's wheel mounted on column with compass in wheelhouse.

The Stump Masts

There are six of these poles, which have derricks attached to them, used in full-size practice for both coaling, boat handling, and any other requirement of hoisting heavy objects aboard. The two foremost poles also acted as funnel stay points for the fore funnel with ringed caps. There are two more sited beside the aft funnel, which likewise doubled up as funnel stays. The final pair were sited at the leading edge of the aft super-structure. They are all at the same height and carried fittings for canvas blast screens. Technically speaking, the two beside the fore bridge stand independently from the foredeck, but because they are a gift in terms of giving firm support to the whole of the platform system, I have used them for structural purposes, adding straps in which retaining screws add rigidity.

This has the advantage that through all the fitting processes to follow, I can disassemble the component parts, and this has proved vital for all the intervening stages. In general terms, it is a very bad idea to fix permanently any item which has serviceable working parts like electric wiring, which may need repair or renewal at some time in the future.

▲ Assembly surrounding the fore funnel. Note supporting stump pole.

Steam Heat

Funnel Steam Pipes Fore and Aft

On the model, before the fore funnel could be finally set up within the masting system, the copper steam pipe had to be added. In full-size practice, the steam pipes were placed abaft the funnels in order to encourage an upward spiral of air around the funnel mouth, helping create a vacuum to draw ambient air up through the funnel spaces more efficiently, and initiate the necessary draught to bring the boilers into full function. The aft funnel, which was much larger in cubic capacity, had two pipes fitted aft, and one in the forward position. The boilers fitted to *Thunderer* numbered eighteen in all, made by the firm of Babcock & Yarrow.

▲ Steam pipe and fittings for aft funnel.

▲ Aft funnel with twin steam pipes fitted aft.

The 60ft Derrick Fittings

Now that the mainmast, forelegs, funnel and platforms can be placed, the question of the masting system as a support to the main 60ft boat derrick has to be considered fully. In full-sized practice, the weights required to be lifted on the sheer-legs of this derrick are very considerable, and must have put a huge strain on the total structure when in action. In common with others, the derrick fitted to *Thunderer* was tubular in form, but there is a photograph in existence, reproduced in May's *The Boats of Men-of-War* (2003), illustrating how the boom of the armoured cruiser HMS *Hampshire* in 1913 failed to lift the necessary weights. Instead of the steel wire giving way, the derrick buckled in half, leaving the picket boat half in and half out of the water.

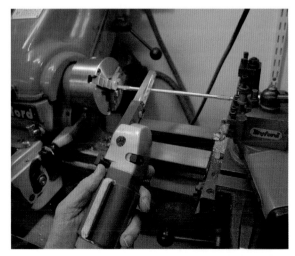

▲ Machining the boat derrick. Hand held linisher and lathe both revolving.

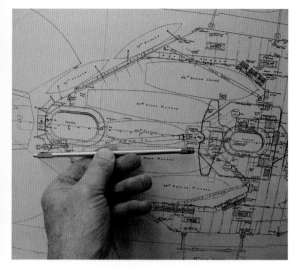

▲ 60ft derrick over the boat deck plan.

▲ Swivel fittings aft the mainmast and boat derrick.

Mainmast Bracket Fixtures

There are four double fixing points on the aft side of the mainmast to support the boom, two of which contain sheaves with cheeks and pivoting housings. The top bracket support has a pivot pin and shackle, and the bottom bracket supports the base of the boom with a universal joint bolted to an axle. The outer end of the derrick has a forked yoke supporting the sheave hoist.

In the hints and tips department, the difficult business of reducing a long thin diameter, like a mast or a boom, is most easily achieved with a motorised rotary file, used in conjunction with the lathe turning at the same time. The two actions are very easy to control, and remove the difficult business of having to fit travelling

steadies on the lathe bed to take the whip out of a long thin piece of stock. This technique of running two machines together replicates the manufacture of the handles on the ship's wheel, and it works equally well with timber, although I have chosen solid brass bar for the derrick in this particular instance.

All the sheaves are pivoted in order that the hoist lines can follow in sympathy, wherever the derrick is swung, and whatever the angle of arc the swing demands. This requires the number two and number three bracket fixtures on the mainmast to be offset at 75 degrees from centre, in order that the hauls can run freely and without interference. In full scale, the electric winches involved with this hoisting and lowering lie beneath the boat deck, on the main deck below. There is no room for them on the boat deck: they would have interfered with the difficult task of getting the boats back into their cradles and chocks. On the model, two counterbalancing weights are fitted below decks in order to keep the hauls tight whenever the boom is moved.

Fixing the brackets has to be done very carefully, and I took the decision to use resin paste rather than risk sweating them on with solder. This method enabled the bearings to be lined up before fixing, and means that this item is a working representation.

▲ Mainmast lug fittings for the 60ft boat derrick.

The Heat Shields

The influence of the hot funnel gases on the original *Dreadnought* tripod mast legs has been much criticised as a serious design fault, particularly with regard to the gun-director's and rangefinder's platforms. Both heat and visibility make it a very uncomfortable position for the critical work required of this team. Under certain conditions the platform was unusable for the heat and smoke generated below. Exactly why the Orion Class of battleships replicated this known mistake is still somewhat of a mystery. It is possible that the answer lies in the relationship of the tripod mast with the necessity of boat hoisting. The inter-relationship of the mast supporting the command structure of the vessel with its platforms and canopy, as well as doubling up as a hoist, is difficult to unscramble, without completely replanning the layout of the boiler and engine rooms, responsible for generating the combusting gases.

On the original *Dreadnought*, steps were taken on the legs of all three masts to minimise the reflected heat transferring to the metal tubes, and heat shields were fitted to disperse the discomfort of hot internal ladder rungs above the canopy, to say nothing of the noxious gases. As these legs were the only way to gain access to the mast platforms above, it had to be possible for crew members to breathe as they clambered aloft. I do not know whether or not they wore protective footwear and gloves.

On the model, the shields were made from brass tube by cutting slots across the tubing, letting in squares of brass sheet after soft-soldering them, filing the tube both internally and externally. As with all heat sinks, the points of contact need to be as small as possible so that the heat is dispersed across the shield itself.

D K Brown, in his book *The Grand Fleet* (1999), records that Admiral Beatty's flagship battlecruiser HMS *Lion*, in the 1909-10 programme, suffered similarly, with the tripod mast supporting the gun-control top abaft the forward funnel. The top was just 39ft 6in from the mouth of the funnel, where gases from the forward ten boilers were vented at a temperature of 550°C. Conditions were intolerable, and this mast was replaced by a pole mast forward of the funnel. HMS *Princess Royal* was similarly modified during completion, at a cost of £68,000 per ship. This would be another good reason for no further changes being made to the design of the Orion Class.

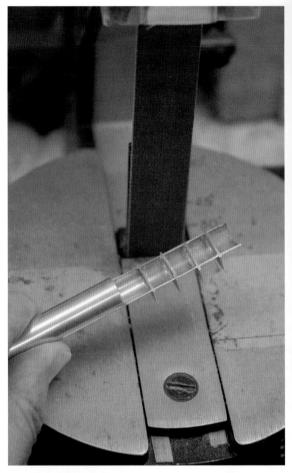

▲ Heat shields for the forelegs.

▶ Shield offered up to plan.

The Former Searchlight Platform

As with so many items on ships, this platform serves several needs. Critically, it is the place where the tripod forelegs join the mainmast, and this joint of the mast struts has to withstand enormous physical strains placed upon it by its many different supporting roles. Thus the need for a collar to tie in the structure: this is an awkward shape, embracing the circle of the three poles splaying out at differing angles. In manufacture it requires much annealing with heat, in order to soften the metal to take the necessary contours. The collar adds mechanical strength and support to the top of the tripod legs. It also strengthens the seat of the fore

▲ The masthead collar.

▲ Preparations for soft-soldering the searchlight platform to the collar.

funnel into the canopy, the 60ft hoisting derrick aft, and counteracts the strains exerted by the tall wireless masting system.

Director Fire Control: The Landing and Gun-Director Platform

In 1912 Sir Percy Scott's director continuous-fire aiming system was adopted as a first by *Thunderer*. This was central gunnery control where one person was in command of firing all the large offensive weaponry as a synchronised salvo. The trigger device was combined with a Mk III Dreyer fire control table, set up in the case of *Thunderer* on the leading edge of the former

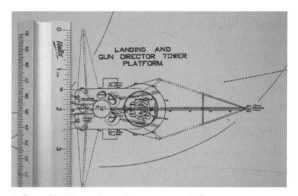

▲ Plan of landing and gun-director tower platform.

▶ The gun-director tower.

searchlight platform, as a new bolt-on in-service addition. It was under-girded from the mast struts, and the lower steaming light was projected forwards onto the V-struts required by the mechanism. In 1912 comparative trials between *Thunderer*, with a fully-developed director system, and *Orion*, without the same advantage, finally demonstrated the value of the director, and eight ships were equipped by the outbreak of war, well ahead of any other navy. The inventor of this calculating nerve centre, Capt F C Dreyer, was one of Admiral Lord 'Jackie' Fisher's original team based at the Gunnery School at HMS *Excellent*, founded at the turn of the twentieth century in Portsmouth.

Dreyer had devised a mechanical computer with precision engineering which was capable of calculating the range of shot, taking into consideration all the necessary information for the accurate firing of all five turrets with a salvo, or with rapid independent firing. This central control represented enormous strides in accurate and effective fire under ideal conditions, but failed miserably when visibility was poor. Some blame is attached to the ineffectiveness of the British capital ships at hitting their targets at long range, typically eight thousand yards, at the Battle of Jutland because the system relied on clear siting picked up by the rangefinders, and in the fog of the North Sea, and the confusion of battle, that was seldom possible.

Fire Control Table

The Dreyer fire control table had fixed to it three essentials: a range plot, a Dumaresq fitted with a range clock, and a bearing plot. In order for it to function fully, it also had to have deflection drums, a deflection totaliser, and a spotting corrector, and it took anything up to twelve people to operate the table, with an additional ten to thirty people assisting in the chain of command.

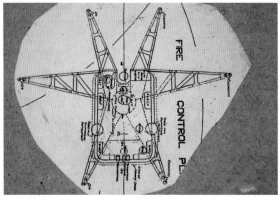

▲ The starfish in profile. Fire control platform is sited above.

▲ MDF pattern for fire control platform. Note metal bar used as form tool.

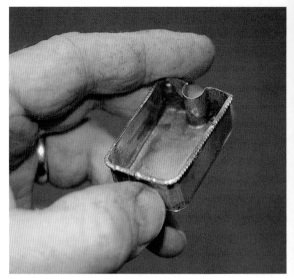

▲ Fire control platform fully soft-soldered.

The Starfish Fire Control Platform

This engagingly-named platform is a metal spreader which gives points of anchorage for the upper masting system. This was the job done in former times by the fighting tops of sailing ships, which provided not only a lookout platform, and an excellent place for sharp-shooting marines, but will also forever be associated with the complications of ratlines, lanyards, futtocks and deadeyes. All of these quaintly-named items had given way to the introduction of steel wire, adjusted by bottle screws, but the platform remained as the prime location for the newest of spotting devices, the rangefinder.

In the confines of the fire control platform, the ship's plans mention not only the word Dumaresq instrument, but also detail two radio transmitters and a receiver, the internal seating arrangements and the 9ft rangefinder itself, manufactured by the company of Barr & Stroud at their extensive factory in Scotstoun, Glasgow. These instruments were successful and reliable, if a little difficult to use, and they remained in service in the Royal Navy aboard all British warships until the advent of radar during the Second World War. The 9ft rangefinder fitted to *Thunderer* was intended for spotting at approximately ten thousand yards; others followed as the demand for extra range grew, but a longer range would have meant altering the dimensions of both the gun-director platform, and the rangefinder platform aft.

On the model, the manufacture of the starfish began

with a pattern from MDF, around which brass strip was formed into the six-pointed star. Incorporated into the star is the heel fixing for the topmast, an awkwardness which needed primary attention, because the necessary U-shape needed to be defined accurately whilst not distorting the total shape. Copper or soft brass wire is the tinsmith's best friend, and that, in conjunction with small bolts, was how the object was held together prior to soldering the star to the platform deck.

With an item like this where the seams have to be soldered, it is better to prepare the surfaces to be jointed with wax flux and small lengths of multicore solder, before introducing an open flame to sweat it all together. This tends to produce too much solder, but that is better than too little. Once again this is soft-solder being used, because too much heat would give distortion to the very thin section of brass being used. Once the central platform was done, the tips were relatively easy to solder and prepare for the eyeplate fixings. The characteristic 'lightening' holes were drilled out with the cone drill, which is designed not to snatch at metal sheet, and is a truly useful tool. The extension piece for the mainmast was soldered into place on the platform, with the advantage that this makes it into a removable and adjustable item.

The fire control platform, or spotting top which houses the rangefinder, is made in a very similar way to the starfish sited below, sharing initially in the difficulty of making provision for the topmast heel without distortion to the enclosure. It also has a handrail which surrounds the basket. This grab-rail would have doubled as a tethering point for the canvas drop from the canopy above. These platforms were normally shrouded against the fierce winds which these high positions had to endure, which is why one normally cannot see much of what is going on, except in model form.

▲ MDF pattern for the starfish.

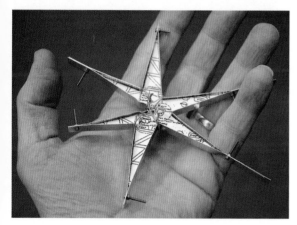

▲ Wired and ready for open flame soft-soldering.

▲ Solder has followed the fluxed seams to the edge of the platform.

▲ Starfish tips soldered and pierced through for eyebolts.

▲ Platform assemblies and anticipation of topmast by use of round file.

▲ Dockside view of mast assembly.

Rounded platform addition for gun-director tower and lower steaming light.

The Sailing Navy Survives

The Main Yard

The Royal Navy is very proud of its traditions, and where those traditions can be preserved, they are. Although this ship has no real need for a traditionally-rigged yard, with foot-ropes, stirrups and horses and jackstay fittings, all these items were familiar to the crew, as a reminder of the training vessels of the sailing navy attached to every naval barracks. Commissioned officers and ordinary seamen alike had been drilled to 'Man the yards,' and it remained a demonstration of courage and fitness to do so.

By 1911 the main function of the yard on a dreadnought battleship was for signalling, and the fiddle halyards for the signal flags were a dominant feature of the masting system. Fiddle halyards are a form of multi-block, whilst halliards are roping lines. At the bunt of the yard is the familiar eighth-squaring, secured to the mast by two chains and hooks in place of the traditional chain slings. The yard is supported by four halliards on the underside of the starfish, and has braces fore and aft, but it is not designed to be lowered or rigged with sail.

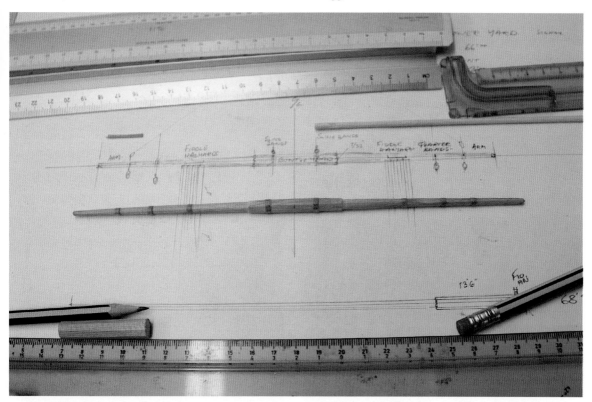

▲ Working drawings for the main yard and topmast.　　▼ Main yard and fittings.

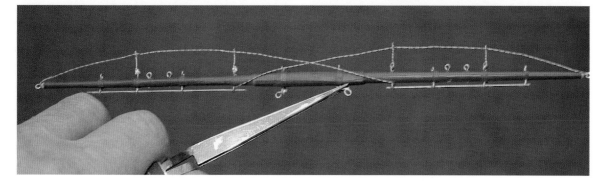

The Topmast

In the early pictures of this class of battleship, very tall masting systems supported experimental aerials in differing configurations of hoops and wires. By 1914 they had all been reduced to a single topmast out of practicality. There was a suspicion that radio transmission was not really suited for ship-to-ship communications, because the orders given could be monitored and picked up by the enemy. Morse and semaphore were safer, tried and tested methods, and a tradition worth preserving. Admiral Beatty, in command of the First Division of battlecruisers, refused to use radio in the Battle of Jutland, and has been severely criticised for losing contact with the fleet as a result.

In line with tradition, the topmast was made of timber, with an eighth-squared heel and fid-pin to keep it chocked in place. Amongst all the steel fabrication on this ship, a wooden mast is perhaps an oddity, but it is difficult to manufacture a tapering steel section, and the rigidity of such a fitting would be unsuited to the whipping motion to which all ships' masts are subjected in high seas. In miniature, this is all good news, except for cutting the mortice through the heel of the mast, which has to be done with a 1mm chisel and a good deal of care.

▲ Topmast yard, planed with spokeshave.

▲ Topmast sheave slot.

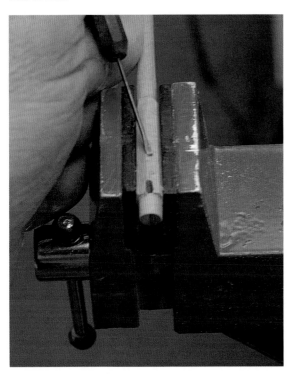
▲ Mortice slot for the fid pin.

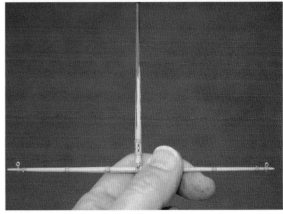
▲ Topmast crossed with yard.

▲ Gooseneck hammered from brass wire.

The Lower Signal Yard

The lower signal yard, which was used for signal halliards in the later and cut-down state of the ship's mast, is a very flimsy item to produce in timber. In order to rig the yard to the mast, it means setting in a sheave to the topmast, which is best done by first piercing the slot from either side with a very fine drill, and then enlarging the drill holes with a file. I use an altered nail file for this procedure, and sometimes this is helped with a clockmaker's screwdriver, finished off with an abrasive strip.

The parrel is made from brass wire, hammered into shape: finally fashion with round-faced pliers for a snug fit to the bunt.

◄ Topmast yard and fittings.

CHAPTER 6

~Ship's Fittings ~

Lights and Lighting

The Aft Bridge Searchlight Platform

Perched on top of the armoured citadel are two platforms: one which supports the four pairs of searchlights, and above that, the aft compass and rangefinder. They are ridiculously beautiful shapes amongst the stark lines of the citadel, as though Edwardian elegance must somewhere be demonstrated in the overall design. Frankly, these shapes derive from contemporary Edwardian furniture design of the Empire style, and in the internal fittings of this ship there were plenty more examples of this kind of craftsmanship, complete with the deep-buttoned leather chairs, desks, and couches.

Tackling a balustraded item like this, in whatever scale, is a test of cabinetmaking skills. The surest way of not splitting the cant edge is first of all to glue the mahogany onto a section of thin 1/32in plywood. You then pierce the item by cutting out the inner section first, following this procedure by reflooring it with a second thin piece of plywood. This gives a recess into which the planks are laid. The floor should be carefully marked so that the laid planks do not stray off centre. The compass platform is made in exactly the same way, with its balustrade which allows the rangefinder to have a 360-degree sweep. When the planking is complete, then the platforms can be cut on their outer edges without any chance of the timber splitting away in the separation process. With careful finishing, the extra thickness of the substrate of ply can be sanded off to give the cant the appearance of solid timber.

The metal supports for the platforms, one looking like a table and the other resembling an ironing board, were fabricated from metal sections of angle and tube, but the real test is to set them squarely in their seatings, because this little tower complex is high profile and very eye-catching. Any deviation is immediately noticeable.

▲ Decking to the cants of the searchlight platform.

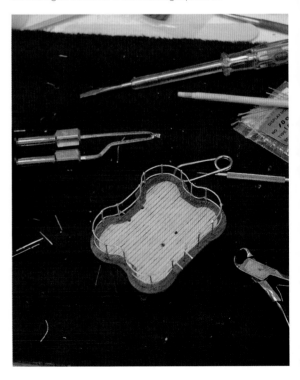

▶ Aft searchlight platform on supporting legs with guard rails.

▲ Metal supports on soldering jig for the aft compass and rangefinder platform.

▲ Lathe turning the swivel base of the rangefinder.

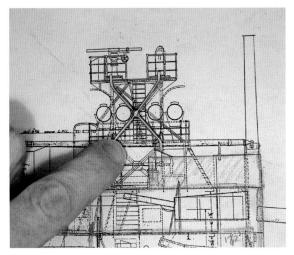

▲ Metal supports offered up to the plan.

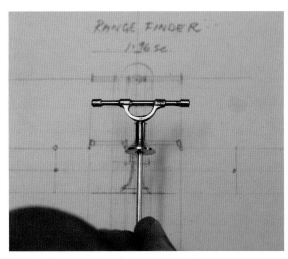

▲ Working drawings for the Barr & Stroud 9ft rangefinder.

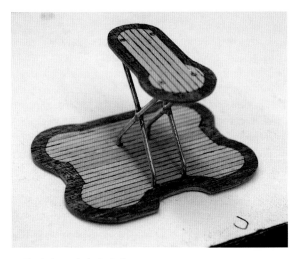

▲ The balustraded aft platforms.

▲ Metal rung ladder leads to the upper platform.

▲ The aft bridge platforms plus aft conning tower.

The Aft Conning Tower

After many challenging tasks involved with details of this ship, this is the one item which gave me the least possible trouble. The tower is a squashed circle which fits into the cleavage of the searchlight tower, with the slit of the gun-siting line just above the super-firing X-turret. It was made from applying pressure to an old imperial-sized copper pipe, capped off with a timber bung and resin paste. Despite the experimental nature of this construction, it is exactly the right shape and size, and I could hardly believe my luck.

Electric Light

There is no doubt that the addition of lighting to any ship, large or small, gives a feeling of being alive and active. It is also a way to display a model which can be very evocative in a darkened room. A conventional 12-volt system was chosen, with a transformer to power the lights. This has the advantage that light bulbs can be replaced into a screw fitting when they fail, whereas LEDs are more difficult if they malfunction. At their present state of development LEDs do not give the quality of light for which I am looking: it is either too white or too blue. I want good side light as well as that rather mellow incandescence of generated DC light, typical of ships and boats in whatever scale. In one

sense, this is the difficult way forward. It means having to make all the light fittings from scratch, and wiring each one up separately with twin flex, so that if one bulb fails, the others continue to function.

The manufacture of the light fittings involved making strips of brass top and bottom, with insulation board in the middle of the sandwich. The screw fittings were achieved by soft-soldering short lengths of 5/32in brass tubing into the brass tongue, tapped with a 4BA thread, to match the light bulb fitting. The positive and negative wires were soldered to the tongues, front and back, with an insulated pin which allows the lights to swivel in a 1/16in tube. The bulbs and fittings are over scale, but they are the smallest manufactured commercially which are both replaceable and reliable.

Wiring up lighting to the extremities of the vessel, finishing with the passage of the twin cable inside 3/32in brass tube, is a demanding job. It was done by first attaching the twin cable to a length of steel wire with quilter's tape, which was then moused up the hull to the stem and stern. A steel guitar string is ideal for this, but insulated garden tying wire will perform the same task. It would be possible to illuminate the whole vessel, including the quarters below decks, and I thought long and hard about this, but I have a caution in mind about the heat generated by these little bulbs. All the steaming lights are free-standing and covered with a brass cowl which disperses the heat. If you touch

▲ Model on signwritten display board.

a naked bulb it will burn you, and that amount of heat in an enclosed space could cause danger if the model were illuminated over a long period of time. This concern would also go for a close-fitting bulb to, for instance, the wheelhouse roof, where there could be a build up of localised heat, which would in its turn damage timber or blister the paintwork in the immediate location.

As things have turned out, the lights produce enough ambient illumination after dark to give the fore portion of the ship plenty of light. In the dark, when all other scale is blotted out, and new shadows are created, the imagination of the onlooker can truly take over, which is an important part of any displayed model.

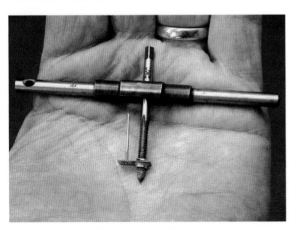

▲ 12-volt DC screw light fitting with 4BA tap.

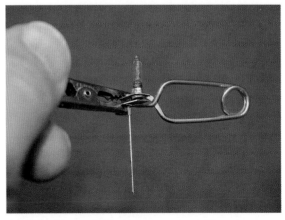

▲ PCB insulator sandwiched between upper and lower brass tongues.

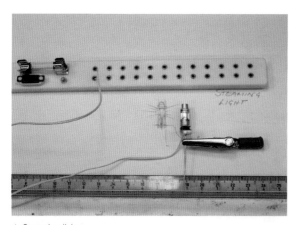

▲ Steaming light.

▲ Night illumination at wheelhouse.

Steaming Lights

Navigation lights have to conform with international regulations in order to prevent collisions at sea. A ship of over 150ft in length must display two white lights, with the second light abaft, and higher than the first, red and green to port and starboard, and a white stern light. *Thunderer* had two positions for two white stern lights used when overtaking. The arc of visibility for the cowls is 225 degrees forward, so all the lights have to be hooded accordingly. The forward anchor riding light, as well as that fitted to the manoeuvring compass platform, would not be lit when steaming.

The Forge, Vice and Anvil

This is a piece of pure indulgence for someone who thinks of himself not as an engineer, but as a blacksmith who works in miniature. In my defence, all three of these items are detailed on the plan of the aft bridge in the positions where I have placed them, and in real life, all three would have been used to repair items which had either jammed, sheared off, needed replacement, or possibly alteration. The presence of the blacksmith's quarters underlines that old adage that if it goes wrong at sea, then there is no one else to fix it.

All three items are diminutives of what appear on my own workbench, and are at the very heart of my workshop. Firebricks are my forge; my engineer's vice is probably Edwardian (I saved it from the dump forty years ago when serving my curacy in Sheffield), and my anvil is ancient, but in constant use. The marks and scars on its face tell tales of jobs long gone, where

▲ Bottle stopper: radical alteration of use.

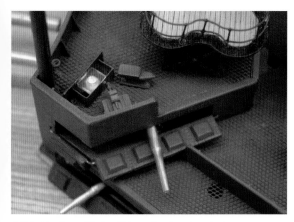

▲ Working forge, blacksmith's anvil and engineer's vice.

hammering has been required for shaping metal into all sorts of configurations. All three items were made from scratch on holiday, with some very basic tools. The oak timber for the anvil was retrieved from a skip – you cannot credit what people will throw away these days.

Lighting the miniature forge was achieved by using an orange plastic bottle stopper, squared off and bored out in the lathe, to accommodate one of the small 12v bulbs. This, unintentionally, gives a bright light in the middle of the forge, as though the coke is white hot, and also illuminates the tread plate below the forge

grate, in an engaging and realistic manner: luck, but very effective at dusk.

Searchlights

Perhaps the most feared of all the possible ways of sinking a ship was night attack by the new breed of German torpedo boat destroyers. These high-powered and fast-moving vessels could in a night raid inflict damage with devastating consequences for battleships and, before the days of radar, the only hope of defence for a ship like *Thunderer* was to be well-equipped with banks of searchlights to spot and destroy these night-raiders with the 4in defensive guns mounted in the two citadels fore and aft. This would require very quick spotting by the searchlight crews to pick out and focus on the aggressors, and split-second reaction for gun crews on watch beside their pivot guns. A top speed for these torpedo boat destroyers was 32.5 knots, carrying eight 20in torpedoes, giving them the ability to outpace their targets by far.

Thunderer was initially fitted with sixteen high-powered carbon arc lamps, rated at 25,000 candlepower each, eight of them arranged by twin mounting on the raised platform of the foredeck and

▼ Searchlights on the fore bridge platform.

on the specified raised deck of the aft citadel. The crew had elevation, training and focus to deal with by handwheels, and the lamps were large enough to be unhandy and difficult to control. Spare lamps were kept below decks in recognition of their vulnerability and need for replacement. The principle on which the searchlights worked was with electrically-energised positive and negative carbon sticks at approximately 50v, with 8-10 amps of current per lamp, according to Sothern's *Notes and Sketches for Marine Engineers* (nd). Striking the arc between the carbon pencils and keeping the gap at a constant distance with the regulating gear meant that these lamps had to be carefully monitored and maintained. Judging by the outer casings, they would also have become as hot as a frying pan.

Anchorage of the Ship

Breakwater

Although the breakwater appears to be a very slim line of defence against the crashing seas encountered in the hostile head winds of the North Sea, it is nevertheless a very distinctive and important feature, separating the anchor cable holders from the forward gun barbettes. The breakwater had to be an efficient way of preventing those mountainous seas from running the full length of the deck, and preventing seawater from finding its way down the many piercings and fittings which a deck has to accommodate. For this reason it is braced with long L-shaped angle brackets, five facing dead ahead, and six smaller ones facing in the outward direction. The shape

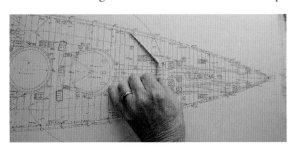

▲ Breakwater over plan.

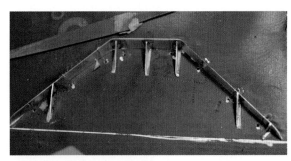

▲ Soldering jig for reinforcing pieces.

▲ Breakwater positioned on deck.

▲ Searchlights on platform aft.

of the breakwater also includes forward rake and gives it great style.

The manufacture of this was not difficult, but required careful fitting in terms of the open-flame soldering process. It was attached to a section of scrap wood, and copper-wired down, so that the brackets could be fitted carefully to the required angles. There is a chance that the wood will catch light from the open flame, but soft-solder runs so quickly that you are more likely simply to scorch the timber rather than set light to it. The top edge is detailed as rounded, and this was achieved by attaching a half-round wooden moulding to the front edge, with a touch of the steaming technique at the outer ends.

The Bower Anchors

The Wasteneys-Smith stockless anchor is not one of the most beautiful anchors on earth, but it does have practicality on its side, and they were fitted to dreadnoughts and super-dreadnoughts alike as standard items. The concept of the Wasteneys patent is very simple. The stock of the anchor has a 'T' cast in one piece at its base. Bored through the T-section, a non-ferrous bar, possibly manganese bronze, passes through the centre of the casting, allowing the two flukes at the crown of the anchor to pivot on a limited arc. The limitation of the arc is controlled by the cast T-piece. This allows free action to the arms and flukes on either axis, and enables the anchor to grip efficiently on the seabed, and stow tightly against the hawse outlet. The two flukes were held captive on the bar by four threaded bolts on each side, which meant that they were both removable and adjustable. At the base of the two flukes are wide flat shoes, enabling the anchor to be hauled off the seabed more easily. These extra lips also had the practical effect

▲ Wasteneys-Smith anchors hove up on starboard quarter.

of toeing the flukes into the seabed when the anchor was laid out on the ocean floor. It is exactly the same action as removing a pair of tight-fitting boots, by using a step or a ledge under the heel.

Stream Anchor

A single close stowing anchor at the stern portside served the needs for mooring aft and manoeuvring ship. It is delineated on the builder's plan as a Byers anchor, similar in many ways to the Martins patent, minus the stock on the shank. It would have weighed in the region of two tons and was weighed by use of the aft capstan. Two small Admiralty-pattern kedge anchors were also stowed amidships for boat and emergency work.

According to Graeme Milne, W L Byers & Co was an important supplier of stockless anchors to local shipbuilders in the period leading up to the First World War, the company being based in Sunderland. One of these anchors has turned up in Sicily where it stands guarding the entrance to Palermo's Arsenal, now converted into a maritime museum. This couples well with the Wasteneys-Smith anchor which stands proudly at the entrance of the UK's National Maritime Museum. They obviously make good door-stops!

▲ Wasteneys-Smith anchor pattern in vice.

▲ Close stowing stream anchor fitted to portside only.

The Second Casting Session

To produce these and the other deck details in this forequarter of the ship required a second and major casting session with the centrifuge. Prior to that, seven fairleads, one cableholder, a pair of searchlights, a capstan pawl rim, a Blakes (bottle screw) cableholder, a deck pipe, a deck eyepiece or lug, three parts of an electric coaling winch and two different sizes of bollards had to be made. Apart from the searchlights, these fittings all represented items involved with anchoring and mooring the ship, and are universal requirements of any vessel of a certain size.

Patternmaking at this level is very pleasurable. All the items not fabricated from brass were carved from boxwood. This precious wood has carving properties which are shared with no other timber, apart from lemonwood, and it is the emperor of carving timbers, favoured for over four hundred years by ship-modellers. Because only one item needs to be made as a master pattern for casting, great care can be lavished on the items in hand. I do coat the timber with French polish, so that the surface is as smooth as possible, which, when it is cast, transfers to looking like a metal finish. A useful tip, given to me many years ago by Magnus Macleod, for finishing enclosed internal shapes such as that encountered by fairleads, is the simple flapwheel. This is a homemade device which involves slitting a barbecue stick for perhaps 2cm, then inserting a glued piece of emery cloth or similar into the slot. The barbecue stick is put into a drill chuck, and the revolving flapwheel will expand and contract according to the size of the aperture, automatically feeling its way without altering the contours.

▲ The pawl rim ratchets being carved into a block of boxwood.

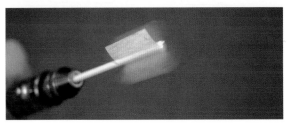

▲ The home-made flap wheel.

▲ The author carving the pawl rim.

▲ The flap wheel polishing the interior of the main fairlead.

▲ The boxwood patterns French-polished and ready for casting.

▲ First pouring of rubber over the Chavant.

▲ The centrifuge and melt pot combination.

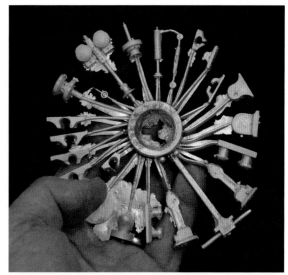

▲ The second casting results.

▲ Cable holders and deck pipes, eye plates and Blakes bottle screw stoppers.

Coaling Ship

Thunderer was one of the last coal burners. By 1915, the Queen Elizabeth Class of battleship had converted totally to oil, and she and her sister ships were the envy of the fleet. Super-dreadnought bunkers would normally stow approximately 900 tons of coal, with a total capacity of 3,300 tons, plus 900 tons of fuel oil. As with her contemporary, HMS *Neptune* (1911), she was equipped with nozzles for burning oil which markedly improved the performance. It was a glimpse of things to come.

All this coal had to be brought to the ship's side in coaling barges, and lifted onto the deck ten sacks at a time using the coaling derricks. The Temperley Transporter assisted in this process of hoisting from the

▲ Assembly of electric coal winches from castings.

▲ Two 'handed' pairs of coal winches plus baseplates.

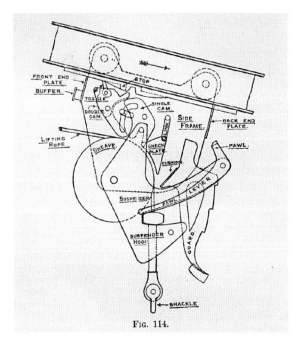

Fig. 114.

▲ The Temperley Transporter. Source: Attwood, *War-Ships* (1906).

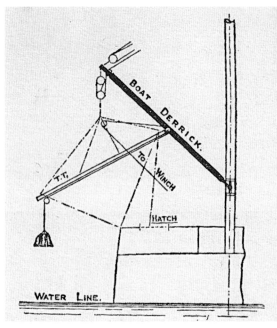

▲ Detail of boat derrick used for coaling ship. Source: Attwood, *War-Ships* (1906).

lighter, linking the purchase to the side-warping barrels of the electric winch. The coal was then barrowed on sack trucks and shovelled into the coal chutes by hand, a job normally carried out by the marines. The worst job was bagging up the lumps of coal into sacks in the barge hold. Overall, it was a filthy job, which covered the whole ship in a film of coal dust and required the efforts of a major part of the ship's company to perform, officers and men working alongside in the roughest kit imaginable. It was often an all-day task, but there are reports that shifting 400 tons per hour was not uncommon, and no doubt there was a competitive element between similar classes of ships for the completion of this job in record time.

Aboard *Thunderer*, and others of the Orion Class, assistance for this arduous and time-consuming task came in the form of six electrically-powered coaling winches, which were sited conveniently close to the bunkers over the fore and aft boiler rooms. These powered winches must have been a great boon in the process of providing fuel for the ship, but I suspect that it was still a back-breaking task for all concerned. Under threat of attack from an enemy, it was vital that this job was literally done and dusted in the shortest possible time.

Detailing these electric winches in miniature

required making the patterns for the component parts of the motor to be included in the second centrifugal casting patterns. These consist of the side-warping barrels and axle, the reduction gearbox, and the main bearing housing and bedplate. There is also a wooden covering for the motor box, and a vertical wheel, which I imagine was some kind of brake. It is of interest to me in a curious kind of way that they are handed left and right on their bases, according to the ship's plans, but not on the huge builder's model of HMS *Monarch* in the Science Museum, which has been so much of a reference point for me throughout the build. Was this a mistake? If it were, it is the only one I have spotted on this otherwise faultless and astounding model at 1:48 scale.

Stanchions

These are properly known as guard stanchions, and were in place to keep personnel, and any item which had broken loose, from being pitched off the side of the vessel. They were designed to be removable, and long lengths of the rails were, in fact, chains, not rod, for ease of access. The guard rails differ in height, and the ones surrounding the upper deck platforms are considerably higher than those surrounding the deck, for obvious reasons of safety.

For some years now, I have overcome the difficult business of depicting these in miniature scale by using a proprietary product fabricated by a man called James Lane. He has in his past been a professional ship-modeller himself, and has developed a system which I can only liken to a two-pronged hairgrip. The section of brass wire used is in half-round, and it is formed with a press tool for the three holes, and then wrapped around at the top to form the miniature upright post.

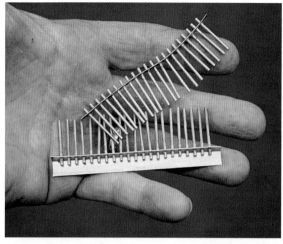

▲ Awning stanchion poles ready for the square bases to be trimmed.

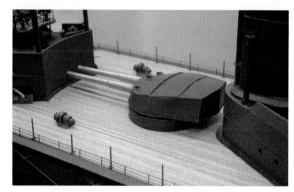

▲ Awning stanchions on their stations.

▲ Awning stanchion with squared bases. Brass tube being sweated with open flame.

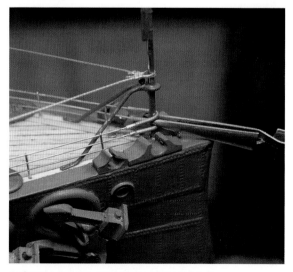

▲ Guard rails being attached around the jackstaff.

▲ Awning line rigged with steel wire.

Scuppers

Scuppers are fitted to the margin planks of the whole decked area in order to drain surface water as quickly as possible, vented away in down pipes from the side walls of the ship.

▲ Deck scupper at foot of breakwater.

Rigging

Rigging the Model

Rigging a battleship of this era needs to be considered carefully. One of the effects of rigging any model ship is greatly to alter the balance of what confronts the onlooker. If the effects are not carefully controlled, rigging can easily take over from all the other detail, viewed now through a web of fine wires, ropes and tensioners. A general caution to all ship-modellers: if this does happen, and all you can see is the rigging and not the ship, then it is almost certainly because the rigging is over-scaled.

The only way to scale rigging properly is to make your own ropewalk, or you will remain a victim of what is available in the shops, or off the reel. This is like telling an artist that he or she cannot mix the paints in the paintbox to get the right effect. A ropewalk allows you to have a huge flexibility of colours and sizes, of left-hand lay and right-hand lay (cable and shroud), and soft and hard materials. These days you are likely to be working in synthetics, but for larger scale models, linen thread is a great personal favourite of mine.

The twentieth century demands steel, or steel-looking, wire, which has its own set of problems, but can be made to look extremely effective using different diameters and production techniques. The result of using metallic wire is that the rigging lines can fade and disappear altogether where the light fails to catch them, which is what also happens in full scale.

The Ropewalk

This machine divides into two parts and can be separated to any desired length. The headstock started out in life as a simple spinning gearbox, with five hooks on five axles, powered by a motor which has forward, reverse and variable speed. The headstock is mains-powered by a captive electric drill, but that is because it is made from bits and pieces. It also needs a foot-switch stop button.

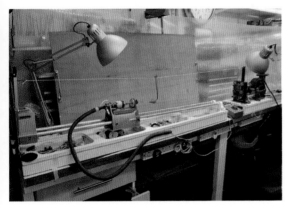

▲ Awning line rigged with steel wire.

Left-Handed or Right-Handed Lay

The headstock is responsible for either left-handed or right-handed lay to the miniature rope. This is important, because you can only lay up strands of rope in the opposite lay to that used by the manufacturer. This means that if the twist in the strand from the supplier is right-handed, the strands will have to be laid up left-handed. The only solution to this problem if you need left-handed lay from a left-handed thread (or vice versa) is to unravel completely the manufacturer's lay, and lay it up the other way. This is where mains power has a big advantage, because the unravelling will involve several hundreds of turns before it tightens up again and reforms

The Headstock

On the headstock, the cogwheels are arranged in a 'sun and planet' configuration, the sun wheel driving the

planet wheels in the opposite direction. The axles have ring hooks attached to them by drilling through the ends, using brass bar for the ring hooks. The gearbox is desperately crude, with brass tube bearings for the axles running through a block of mahogany. The only thing to be said in its favour is that it is over thirty years old now, and has spun literally miles and miles of rigging lines.

▲ The headstock.

▲ The tail stock and the 'top'.

The Tailstock

The tailstock is powered by a DC motor, combined with a 12v transformer, originally designed for model railways. Fine control is necessary at this end for serving (wrapping) threads, and for putting twist into the ropemaking process, known technically as 'rope hardening'.

The machine has two other secrets. The first of these is a fisherman's double-ended spinner, which is what the threads are attached to in the initial stages of the ropemaking process. The second secret is a sliding carriageway, which compensates for the fact that when rope of any diameter is being spun, it will shrink and will pull itself towards the headstock. I am using an old electric drill holder for the sliding carriage, and two parallel bars, which allow the whole tailstock to slide by friction, and has the added advantage that when you are threading up, everything can be held gently in tension

several thicknesses of strands being spun together, but at larger scales the difference is very apparent, and it is the sort of thing which judges and professionals will pick up. Hawser ropes, which are four-stranded, look hugely effective.

The Process
The strands are tied onto the hooks at the headstock

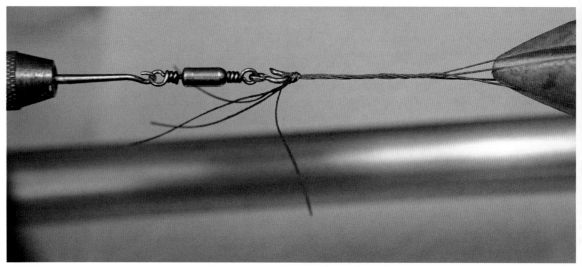

▲ Left to right: fixed hook in the chuck, the spinner and hook to which the strands are attached.

by simply pushing the tailstock to the left-hand end.

There are two separate cone shaped tops. One has three grooves sawn into the cone, and the other four. The grooves are always kept waxed, and are used for laying up either three or four strands of roping. Their function is to keep the threads separate when they are being spun by the gearing from the headstock. The cone is miraculously squeezed along the rope line as it is formed, and it will run automatically on an overhead line, or it can simply be controlled by hand.

How Does It Work?
As mentioned above, rope depends on the 'lay' of the strands. Most modern synthetic polyesters are right-hand lay, which means that when you come to spin them together they must be laid up left-handed. This is why it requires a motor at the tailstock end with a reverse facility. If left-hand lay is an issue, untwist the manufactured lay on the ropewalk, and lay it up on the opposite hand. This takes a surprising amount of turns, during which the tension will need to be hand-adjusted at the tailstock end as the strands become unravelled. The rope then re-tensions of its own accord. At 1:96 it is very difficult to tell the difference, unless there are

and walked down to the tailstock. The tailstock motor has a revolving hook set in a small chuck. To that fixed hook, the fisherman's double-ended spinner is attached, with a further small hook at the leading end of the spinner. Into the spinner hook, the first strand is threaded, followed by however many others are to be laid up together. They are then knotted together at the tailstock end. The effect of this is that the driving hooks at the headstock will now be able to spin the threads in on each other, which will have the effect of holding the separate strands together by its own inbuilt tension.

Insert the Top
Before the headstock motor is switched on, the grooved cone of the top is inserted, so that it will separate the individual threads until such time as the twisting tension squeezes the top towards the headstock. At first nothing happens, but when the tension builds, the top will move rapidly along the roping line, and as it comes to the headstock, the foot switch cut-off will need to be used.

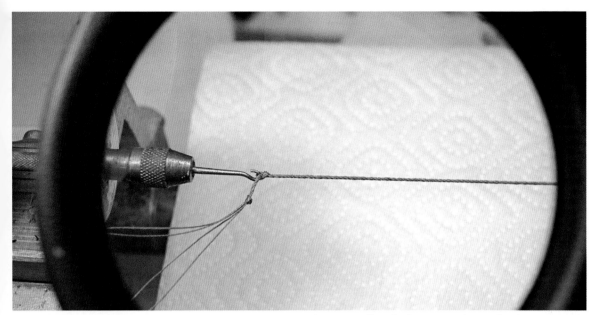

▲ The rope is hardened by removing the spinner, and hooking the rope onto direct drive from the tailstock motor.

The End of the Process

The miniature rope is now formed, but not hardened. The hardening process puts extra strength into the rope by twisting the newly-made rope from the tailstock end, like wringing out a wet towel.

By removing the fisherman's spinner or, as I do, hooking the spinner onto the fixed hook, the whole rope is now spun together, squeezing the tension up from the tailstock. This will see the tailstock carriage on the move again as the tension increases. In larger scales you can see the threads tighten together, and you can hear the motor strain as this happens. In the past, when ropes were made by hand, this was the blood vessel bursting process which ropemakers went through on the ropewalk, which was a truly tough job.

The rope can now be cut off and used, and only now will you know the final diameter. This depends on how tightly the rope has been spun and hardened, and is not a simple calculation of multiples of the strands involved.

Where rope looks most effective on a model is when it is matched against other samples: the three-stranded against the single strand, or the thickness of a served backstay against a thin ratline.

Steel Wire

The standing rigging of a twentieth-century battleship is relatively simple compared with its nineteenth-century counterpart, but it is not so simple in small scale, because you cannot use steel wire on account of its tension. I have used steel wire for the awning

▲ Spun rope, left-hand laid. Note how well it miniaturises.

▲ Steel rope under direct drive from tailstock for rope hardening.

stanchion lines, but it has far too much tension for rigging to masts and yards on a model. The solution was found in a Coats metallic 60% polyamide and 40% metallised polyester thread, code 301. I purchased this as a standard item with no fuss in a local milliner's shop. Also worthy of note for more traditional rigging is Guttermans 100% linen thread, produced in some very good dark colours, but by way of warning, linen thread is disappearing off the face of the earth as a readily available product.

The Coats metallic is a monofilament with a wrapping of silver around the core. It is right-hand laid. Three strands wound into a steel rope comes out under tension at 0.32mm or 0.012in. At 1:96 scale, this is equivalent to 1.25in, which is slightly under scale, and therefore highly desirable. It is also far too bright a colour of silver, but this is easily dealt with in the usual manner, by coating it with French polish shellac, or a dark varnish, just to kill off the shine. A tip worth knowing is to have a short length of metal U-channel which can act as a small reservoir for the French polish or varnish. Run the angle behind the thread while it is under tension, dragging a small brush along it at the same time. This method gets the varnish all around the thread, and is much easier than trying to paint it *in situ*.

Bottle Screws

I now make these by using a very fine section of aluminium pipe, which is prepared by shallow-grinding the ends and simply threading through the made wire, looping it down and back for the hook, and crimping it in the centre with fine-nosed pliers. This holds it all in place, and makes an unobtrusive fixture which is quick and easy to manufacture.

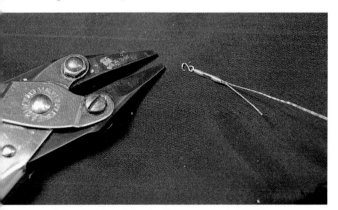

▲ Bottle screw. Note how the wire is fed through the hook and returns to be crimped.

The Aerials

These hooped antennae are a bit of a challenge, and need to be made with extreme care. At the outset I was doubtful about how to set these up successfully. Should they be done *in situ*, or away from the model, and what kind of tension was going to be involved at the masthead with four of them pulling against each other? I reasoned that the experiment would be best done away from the model, and that control of the tension was best conducted on a small, makeshift loom.

▲ Aerial hoops cut into matching rings.

The Copper Hoops

These hoops need to be very light, with fine, evenly-spaced holes around the circumference, which are not going to fray the silver wire wrapping. The hoops are first formed by twisting two lengths of copper wire in a handheld brace. The spun wire is then cut off and wrapped around a piece of bar or dowel. A cut with a pair of tin snips along the length of the bar produces the rings, which can then be soft-soldered

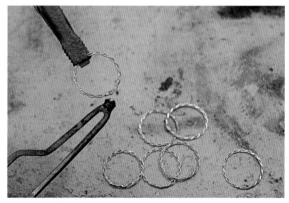

▲ Hoops flattened with hammer to open the weave and soldered at the joint.

▲ The loom.

▼ The tourniquet.

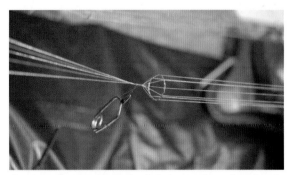

together. The technique used for making the holes is the old jeweller's trick of twisted wire, hammered flat. The very gentle hammering process opens the twist in the wire, through which the antennae can be made to pass. The fact that they are really slots, rather than holes, allows the line-up process a little latitude, which is a good thing. The holes are also rounded, rather than sharp, preventing the vibrations, which will always be a part of this set-up, from fraying the lines.

The Aerial Loom

Eight small picture screw-eyes were centred into two separate blocks of wood set between two vices. This arrangement allowed for altering the tension and keeping the lines taut. Cyano glue was used to set the copper rings in place, followed by a tourniquet which brought the wires together into a cone shape. This procedure was followed by the combined aerial wires being twisted together to form a central core of rope, which in its turn was glued along its length. What worried me initially was the amount of tension this was all going to put on the topmast and the wireless telegraphy yard.

Wireless Telegraphy Yard

Alarmed by the apparent tensions involved, I decided to make the wireless telegraphy yard out of brass bar, and solder all the fittings, so that there could be no nonsense concerned with the pull which I now knew was going to be exerted at the masthead. My other concern was that the miniature antennae lines would twist uncontrollably, which is the reason for the intro-

duction of a short length of chain on the tethered ends of the aerials. Chain, very usefully, can be tensioned to counteract twist in thread, which often happens with ship models that have long lengths of rigging.

Finally, all rigging lines need a way of drawing up the tension: this is best done by having two ends joined by a short length of cordage or lanyard, which can be

▲ Wireless telegraphy yard and collar made from brass rod.

▲ The wireless telegraphy yard, rigged with aft aerials. Note how the aerial wire disappears.

slowly adjusted up and secured. This is how the tensions were finally aligned and matched, bringing these very high profile items to a sufficient tautness to make them look presentable and, hopefully, not drawing too much attention to themselves.

Radio Waves

Please do not enquire from me how these antennae actually worked. I have already admitted to being of the mind that radio-control is nothing other than pure magic, but I have read a simple explanation in Stuart Ballantine's *Radio Telephony for Amateurs* (1922), an illustration that has enlightened me somewhat. This could be because it uses the analogy of a pond.

He asks his readers to imagine the smooth surface of a pond being disturbed by throwing a stone into the middle, and ripples forming which spread out along its surface in a series of miniature water waves. The waves travel with a velocity of a few metres per second, and carry with them energy capable of setting into motion a small distant floating object. He then asks the reader to imagine that the stone is the transmitter, the distant floating object is the receiver, and the water is replaced by the ether.

As far as I can detect, the hooped aerials intercept that energy coming through the ether with greater efficiency than a single or dipole antenna, giving the receiver and the transmitter more output and gain. Marconi's research with radio transmission is equally matched by his successful experiments with aerials and increases of range with his quarter wave monopole, later to become known as the Marconi aerial.

▲ Complete antennae system rigged fore and aft.

Flags and Flagmaking

The White Ensign is worn by His or Her Majesty's ships of war in commission. The size of a British Ensign flag is commonly expressed in terms of breadths of 9in, and in the Union flag, the length is twice the breadth. The standard size is 16 breadths in height by 32 breadths in length, which translates into a flag measuring 12ft x 24ft. Each cloth of bunting has a few thicker threads not only into its edges, but also every 6in of its warp, and this mark shows the bunting to be of Government make.

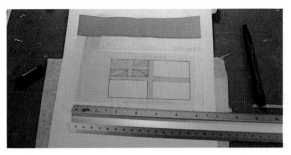

▲ The White Ensign. Cotton voile stretched over the pattern and marked out.

Hoisting and Hauling Down the Colours

According to the *Manual of Seamanship*, HM ships in commission, when at anchor in home ports and roads, shall hoist their ensigns at 0800 from 25 March to 20 September inclusive, and at 0900 from 21 September to 24 March inclusive; when abroad, at 0800 or 0900 as the Commander-in-Chief shall direct. Ensigns are to be hauled down at sunset. Ensigns are also to be worn at sea, when there is sufficient light for them to be seen, but may be hauled down when out of sight of land and other ships. The Union Flag is worn by HM ships of the Royal Navy at the jackstaff in harbour between the hours of 0800 or 0900 until sunset, unless the ship is refitting.

▲ Rotating the board to keep sharp edges on the tip of the paintbrush.

Flagmaking

In order to make an atmospheric flag in miniature, it is a good idea first to study how flags appear and behave in full size. There are several possible interpretations, depending on how light falls on a flag. If viewed with the light shining onto the cloth bunting, it will appear as a fluid, solid colour. If seen from the opposite side, against the sunlight, the cloth will appear grainy, and less evenly coloured, and on a large ensign the stitching lines of a properly-made flag will show.

▲ Allowing the grain of the cloth to breathe. Note allowance for wiring at the edge.

All of this is influenced by the way cloth flies in the wind, and it will, more often than not, adopt a snakelike movement as the wind passes on both sides of the bunting. The fact that it is constantly on the move is what makes a large flag slightly hypnotic, and in the course of history, flags and banners are what have led men into battle against the foe, and have been the signal for victory or defeat.

Apart from national pride, I believe that a good deal of time and effort needs to be expended on flagmaking, and I have in the course of my travels seen many models let down badly by ensigns which have either

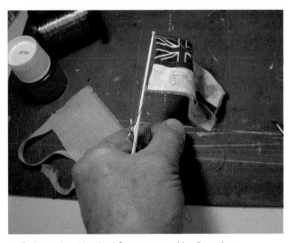

▲ Ensign pole with wired flag on top and leading edge.

been bought and stuck on, with almost no further consideration given to them, or crudely made compared with the rest of the model.

Painting the Flags

I use fabric paint, which is a thermofixable paint that works best on a material such as cotton voile. It will work on manmade cloth, but it takes more naturally to translucent, soft cotton material. A rectangle of this material needs to be ironed flat and stretched over a board, with a scaled pattern under the cloth, ready for the lines of the flag to be drawn. A fine point 0.3mm indelible ink pen is used to mark out the flag, and when fully delineated, the cloth is then laid over absorbent material, such as kitchen towel, and painted in with the appropriate colours.

It is very important when painting in to rotate the whole board, so that the sharp angles which present themselves can be painted with the tip of the brush, and not the backside of it. It goes without saying that you need good quality brushes for this, and not the old faithfuls which no longer point up as they should. The technique of turning the board will give you sharp edges and fine lines from the brush tip. Between the application of each colour the cloth is dried off with a blast of hot air from a hairdryer, or left to cure naturally. This will prevent any bleeding of one colour into another. When it comes to the large blocks of colour, and particularly the white, only paint to the edges, leaving a certain roughness to the texture of the cloth in the middle. If you paint it all in, it will make it all too solid-looking, and this shading effect helps with catching the light when it is supposedly flying in the wind.

Realism

To give a miniature flag the ability to have some realism, the trick is to wire the leading and top edges with copper wire folded into the material along the outer edge and glued with a contact adhesive. In real life, the leading edge of a flag is invariably pulled into a crescent shape, which can be mimicked at this point. It also gives a flag character if some of the ends are frayed,

which can be done by pulling out the warp and weft of the weave at the bottom and trailing edges. Make sure, too, when the flag is being rigged, that the head of the flag appears at the truck of the staff; any hint that the sheave is lower down the ensign staff is an abhorrence to naval practice. The toggle should touch the truck. The final trick to flagmaking is to apply the dirt which is the gift of a coal-fired ship to every bit of bunting. Button-polish shellac will do this in just a few strokes of the brush, giving it that used look, which marries the flag into the model rather than it being an appendage standing on its own.

▲ Ensign in place. Note the frayed edges of the cloth.

CHAPTER 7
~ *Nearing the End: Auxiliary Craft* ~

Ship's Boats

Big ships and small boats share the same anatomy. Their backbones are referred to as keels, their frames are known as ribs, and their planking systems are often referred to as the skin. They have heads, knees, breastbones, buttocks, arms, knuckles, forelegs and feet, and that is only a beginning. The small armada of auxiliary boats which every battleship carried was essential for the day-to-day smooth running of the mother ship, and had little to do with lifesaving capacity although, *in extremis*, this role could be fulfilled. The real reason for so many different kinds of boat on display was the result of the deep draught of the modern battleship requiring them on many occasions to be moored at some distance from the shoreline or harbour station. Every item of supply that needed to come aboard on a daily basis arrived by ship's boat, and each shape and size of boat was more or less suited for the intended work.

The boats also had a secondary role of providing an endless source of naval evolutions to be carried out, which not only trained young men in seamanship, but also kept up the routine of fitness and challenge for all members of the ship's company. It was often the case that competitions and races were arranged between similar ships, and the popularity of this friendly rivalry was a great boost during the long hours, sometimes weeks or months, of waiting for action.

Two matters which were common to all ships' boats in the Royal Navy were pride and protection. Aboard *Thunderer*, these boats were given the highest order of protection possible, housed in the armoured citadel between the tripod mast and the main funnel, protected by blast walls from shot and shell. The smartness of appearance and good order of these boats was the mark of the particular ship to which they belonged, and a barometer of the crew's morale. The difficult drill of 'Out boats' was rehearsed and practised to perfection, without damage to the paintwork or any sign of injury to the vessels, and brightwork on the brass fittings of the steam boats would be polished on a daily basis.

The plans of *Thunderer* depict the full complement of ship's boats, including two 50ft steam pinnaces, a 42ft sailing launch, 36ft sailing pinnace, three 32ft cutters, four 27ft whalers, a 30ft gig, and a 16ft dinghy, or jolly boat. I am only detailed to make a token sample of this full complement, with the sure knowledge that at any one time in the life of the mother ship there would be variations and absentees. There is also a practical detail on the model regarding access to the radio-control receiver housed beneath the boat deck, so that only two boats rather than five will be placed within the casemate walls.

The 32ft Cutters
The 32ft cutters, which in real life were on permanent duty, were hoisted on radial davits amidships. In an emergency of any kind these would be the first boats to be

▲ Solid block of jelutong, from which the cutter will be carved, with half-plan marked on the centre line.

▲ The flexicurve used for clear delineation of hull plan view.

▲ The bottom one-third being bandsawn from the top two-thirds.

▲ Table set at 25 degrees for the inside profile cut.

lowered on to the water, a drop of some fifty feet below.

In full size, the construction of these cutter boats used clinchered planks, which was the lightest constructional method then available, made in the workshop over a basic frame, where the strakes overlap one another and lines of copper nails clench the planks together on their leading edge from stempost to sternpost. The form of the hull is then internally braced and strengthened with ribs rather than frames because the shape is dictated by the lapping of the planks. The larger boats used the alternative method known as carvel build, where the planks butt up against one other, and are caulked along their seams with tarred rope to make them watertight. Their shape is dictated by framing, and strengthened between the frames by further ribs. This leaves a smooth surface on the exterior of the hull, which is easier to repair, but makes for a heavier construction overall. The heavier boats were also often double diagonally planked for even greater strength.

Working at a scale of 1:96, I used a carving technique for both of these styles on account of their small size. Model ships and boats of the twentieth-century period in major museums are, in the majority of cases, carved rather than built. Even the large builder's models of the late nineteenth and early twentieth century use a style of what is called 'bread and butter' to describe hulls which are carved from a hollowed-out sandwich of planks placed on top of one another, glued together, and carved to shape on the outside with great care using external templates. Shipyards also used half-models to work out the plating lines, and the shift of butts.

The programme begins with choosing a good piece of carving timber. There are several which could be used, but a tight grain with no appreciable knots or flaws is essential. I use jelutong, and so do many other model shipwrights, but I have also used boxwood and tulipwood in the past; English lime is another favourite.

The plan view of a vessel is the overhead image. The profile plan is the side view and the view end-on is known as the body plan. This gives the builder the three dimensions needed, but often the only plans available are the plan view and profile, which is the case here. Once again, these plans come from *The Battleship Dreadnought* (2001) by John Roberts. The image of a boat is normally only drawn as a half-view, so that the constructor will need first of all to measure and draw the keel line onto the block of wood to be carved, and reverse the half image, drawing with a pencil carefully around the profile. There is a drawing instrument, known in this country as a flexicurve, which is very useful in this work for defining curvature. The curve from the drawn image will stay put whilst you draw in the line, giving much better definition than a line drawn freehand. Using an engineer's set square, also draw in the block lines at the top and sides. The next move is to make two cuts along the length of the block of wood. The first cut is to separate the timber from the block and the second is to make a one-third and two-thirds cut line. The one-third piece, which is the thinner of the two, will be the bottom of the boat, and the two-thirds will be the side walls.

This technique is really reversing the normal procedure for boat building by concentrating on the inner rather than the external profile. The inside is the difficult piece to bring into shape, because the grain in the wood goes through 360 degrees. Using a spoon gouge, which is the only tool which could fetch out the shape with predetermined accuracy, is not an easy option on such a small scale. Nor is this situation helped by not being able to clamp a rounded hull in a vice for any carving activity. What is required is a fretsaw blade in conjunction with an angled table. I used a powered scroll saw set over to an angle of 25 degrees. The cut line is continuous and will leave an inner piece, shortly to be used as a holding device, between clamped jaws when carving the hull bottom, so the inner sawn shape should be put on one side and kept. Even with a scroll saw, the operator should steer clear of the marked line, and finish to the pencil line with a file or rasp. If powered tools are not available, then simply use a brace and bit auger to take out the middle space and finish to the internal line at 25 degrees with a coping saw.

There is now a flat hull bottom to join to the sides. If the constructor wishes to give extra depth to the hull bottom, a spoon gouge can be used to hollow out the bottom before rejoining it and clamping up with glue but given the fact that all hulls have to have flooring in place which will be covered over with the bottom boards, this is not really necessary.

The hull is now taken out of block form by sawing close to the outer profile; a bandsaw is ideal for this work, but it can be done by hand. Machinery only speeds things up, something which has to be taken seriously by those working on commission, but it should never stop or be a discouragement to those who

▲ Inner profile cleaned up with a needle file.

▲ The inner piece is retained for clamping up.

▲ The top and bottom reunited.

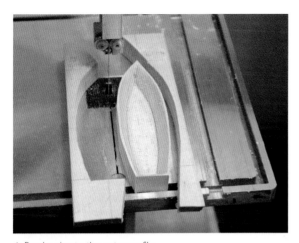

▲ Bandsawing to the outer profile.

▲ Carving out the deadrise at the stern with half-round needle file.

▲ Linishing off the outer profile.

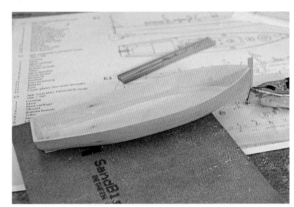

▲ Hull of the admiral's barge: note the square foot of the stempiece.

▲ The hull clamped up with the inner piece, prior to carving.

▲ Sawing the keel with Japanese drawsaw.

work completely by hand. Machinery is very good for knocking things into shape, but lines on ships and boats are so subtle that only hand work will bring any item to completion. That being said, you will have noticed throughout this book the pivotal role played by the strap linisher. This is the machine tool which, above all others, I now regard as indispensable, and here it is again used for finishing the hull exterior to the all-important sheer line of the boat.

The inner section can now be seen to fit inside the hull, giving it firm support whilst the rasping of the bottom is undertaken. The cheap, but very useful, ball-jointed swivelling table vice is ideal for this sort of operation. Boat hulls have streamlining in the form of a scallop shape removed at the stern, and also in the swell of the planking towards the stem on the turn of the bilge. On the 32ft cutters the hull lines are more stubby, as compared with the shape of the 42ft launch, for instance; greater length allows for a better flow line and improved hydrodynamics, but these shapes can only be tackled with a concave, half-round file or rasp. There is also a carver's finishing tool called a riffler file: these come in all sorts of weird shapes, but the half-round file is the tool of choice, and with this tool the hull is shaped and refined. Be encouraged at this point. The hull is defined and the lines of carving between the stem and stern will naturally lead towards one another as the sanding and finishing take place; the work is very pleasurable.

The next big visual improvement is the addition of the keel and stem. This requires a saw cut to go straight down the bottom of the hull and follow round to accommodate the stempost. Cutter boats have rounded stems for ease of handling on shorelines and so forth. The squarer foot of the launch indicates that these larger boats required a quayside, having a significantly greater draught than the hoisting boats. The initial saw cut is made with a Japanese drawsaw, a super-sharp saw which is drawn towards the operator, and if you have not tried one of these you will not appreciate the difference the direction of pull rather than push makes. All these years and the Western hemisphere got it wrong! The over-fine cut line for the keel is then enlarged with a small metal hacksaw inverted in the vice, running the hull up and down the hacksaw blade, and finishing on centre around the curvature of the stem, checking carefully on the progress as you go. There is a need to carve the stempiece (mine came from a lollipop stick) and then join a keel piece to it and

▲ Opening up the width of the saw-kerf with metal hacksaw.

▲ Addition of the stempiece to the 32ft cutter.

plane it all down to size. As though by magic, the boat is given style and substance, and this stops the miniature hull looking like half of a wooden handle.

The addition of rubbing strakes and a top wale in which the squared rowlocks are carved add character and define the vessel and its external appearance. Internally, the ribs need to be included, and the tip here is not to try to do this with timber strip, which is very difficult to control and lacks the half-rounded look of real ribs, but to use string or thread which has been dipped in a wood glue. Drag the threads through a blob of wood glue and apply them directly with a pair of tweezers. The two strips of wood which overlay the ribs horizontally are called risers, and they support the thwarts. These seats

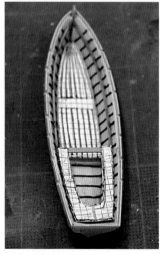

▲ The inner detail of frames, seat risers, etc, in 32ft cutter.

▲ Fixing the knees to the thwarts.

▼ Interior detail of 32ft cutter: note the bottom boards and gratings.

for the oarsmen which straddle the boat are an important part of its strength and structure; the word comes from athwartships.

The really tricky bit of making these boats look truly realistic is fixing the knees to the thwarts. There is a varying angle of contact between the knees and the gunwale of the boat: more oblique at the central portion of the boat than the extremes. These knees take ages to cut, trim and fix. They are held with superglue, and the recommendation is to use the thicker, thixotropic sort, which gives a racing chance of setting them at the correct angle. The top edge does not matter too much as they are going to be ground off with a miniature stone in the form of a cone, but the angle and point of contact is critical. Once you have seen the knees finished and in place, it does set the boat off into a category of true realism. Also required are the bottom boards and the mast fittings for the times when these vessels were sailed rather than rowed. Gratings also add character, and are made from fine embroidery linen with fourteen holes to the inch.

The Captain's Jolly Boat

The beauty of this system of making small boats is that it applies to all shapes and sizes. I have even been able to make the captain's jolly boat out of original timber from what was left of *Thunderer*'s deck, discussed in Chapter 3. It is a mere two inches in model length and made from teak.

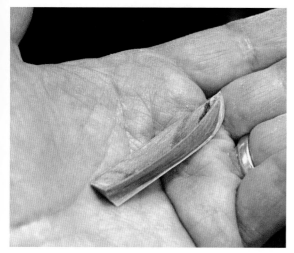

▲ The diminutive captain's jolly boat – made from original teak from the deck of HMS *Thunderer*.

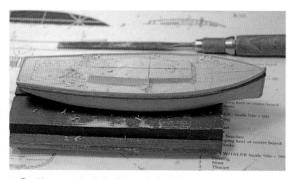

▲ Decking over the hull of the admiral's barge.

▲ The finished admiral's barge.

The Admiral's 40ft Barge

The admiral's 40ft barge, although decked over and scale-planked, was built using the same technique as the cutters, and with its internal cabin gives the feeling of depth to the hull, which is where so many carved boats fail to convince. However, be aware that there is not a lot of flesh on the bone in some places with these carved hulls. Always use the old violinmaker's test if in doubt: hold it up to the light to check the thickness of all parts when sanding or filing down. If the light shines through, then you are in trouble.

The Whalers

The 27ft whalers, with their double ends, have an almost jaunty appearance, and introduce the thought that the sheer line is best worked into the block model before any external lines are cut. This sweep is more easily removed at the outset when the shape is still in block form, and it increases the accuracy of the inner profile at the centre of the hull if the sheer has been previously carved. In other words, if you do not take the sheer out when the hull is still in block form and has been sanded to the outer profile, there will be a very slight thickening of the top wale when you file or sand the hull walls down. If you carve the sheer first, and then apply the pattern or drawn profile, this will not happen.

Other than this detail, the principles for construction remain the same as for the other boats. Whalers, although they appear as if they could be stowed one inside another, had fixed thwarts which prevented this from happening, but their manoeuvrability and general handiness made them one of the most useful boat types available, proven by the fact that there were more whalers than any other type of ship's boats. They made lively sailing craft with their twin masts raked aft and their iron drop keels, lowered from the centre box.

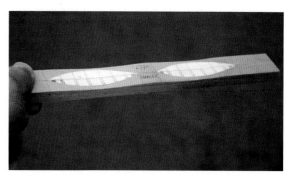

▲ Whalers with the sheer taken out before being carved.

▲ Whalers half-built: note the gratings and the single crutches along the gunwale.

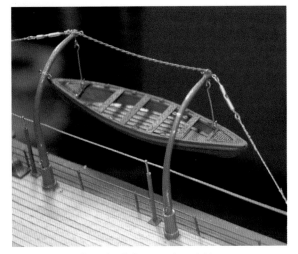

▲ Whaler slung from the davits on starboard side.

▲ The chock pattern.

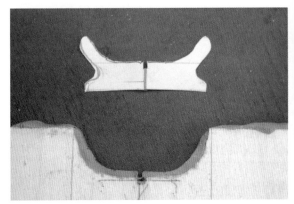

▲ The body line of the hull copied onto a paper pattern.

Boat Chocks

With the two major model ship's boats built, they now need to be safely secured on the boat deck, and this is done with the boat chocks; they are constructed to support the individual hulls in an upright position. As the name suggests, these were originally just elongated triangles of wood which were malleted under the ship's boats to keep them in place on the skids, but here the situation is of a very different order, in terms of weight and safety. A fully-engined and equipped launch or barge would be a weighty item. An unladen 42ft cutter weighed over 8 tons, and so the need to make it fast would be of paramount importance. The secondary consideration would be that the vessel should be cradled in such a way as not to harm the hull when out of the water.

Chocks are not easy: they have to fit a hull at a very precise point fore and aft, and also be of sufficient thickness to support the hull, spreading the pressure on the boat's timbers and frames as widely as possible. The

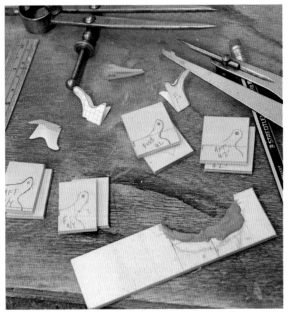

▲ The half-patterns made up in pairs.

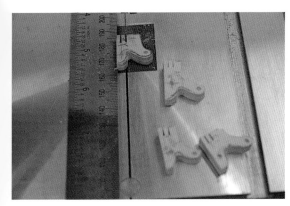

▲ Saw cuts being made for veneer joints.

final requirement of the chocking structure is that it is bolted down to the deck through the feet, to prevent the secured vessel from coming adrift. In order to overcome the difficulties of a precise fit for each chock, a simple jig should be constructed, which can be used for all the required profiles, and is basically just a generalised hull shape which is lined with plasticine. When the hull is pressed into this shape, it will impress a very precise profile. The plasticine impression is knifed off on both sides of the profile, giving the draughtsman an image which can be copied onto squared paper.

Careful study of the impression will also show the

camber; the camber is the measure between the front edge of the profile and the back edge, which will be appreciably different according to the thickness of the timber used for the chock, because the hull shape alters drastically at the points of contact at the extremes of the vessel. In practice, a little bit of filing with a half-round file will solve the issue, but go gently to ensure that you are improving the fit, rather than ruining it.

Once a satisfactory paper image has been arrived at, a half-pattern of the point of contact with the hull bottom can be cut and transferred onto presawn squares, exactly as the original frames of the ship were treated, with the squares pinned together using wooden dowels before being cut out as a pair. This may seem like a lot of trouble for such simple items, but unless they are made in matching halves, it is nearly impossible to guarantee that they will be perfect images of one another. The last machining process is to join them by cutting a pair of saw slots into the upright faces, using scraps of veneer to fix them together mechanically.

If you wish to seal the outer edge of the plywood chock, flood it with superglue. This seals the end grain of the plywood and, with a little sanding and the application of paint, will give the appearance of solid timber.

▼ The chocks accurately cradling the hull shape.

Victualling in the Royal Navy

On the starboard side opposite X-turret is a note of instruction on the shipyard plans for a special davit for hoisting carcasses of meat aboard. 'Socket for davit for embarking beef' is the official description for this all-important task. Officially, every man aboard was to receive as a daily ration, 1lb of meat, either beef or pork. When supplies of fresh meat ran out, the meat held in reserve would have been salted down to save it from putrefaction.

A slaughtered carcass of beef weighs approximately half a ton, providing about 250kg of edible meat for around 550 men, so that this davit would have been in constant use in harbour service for the importation and hauling of this vital source of food and energy. It was supplemented on a daily basis with small amounts of biscuits, rum, sugar, tea and 1oz of chocolate, and when available, soft bread and fresh vegetables from the victualling yards. When these ran out, the diet consisted of split peas, salt beef, flour, suet, currants and raisins according to Captain John Wells' book, *Immortal Warrior* (1987). This list comes originally from the days of the sailing and steaming navy, but the diet and the way it was cooked and administered altered very little until a major review of the Navy's dietary needs and its distribution. This led to the introduction of what was called the 'general mess system', the first trial of which was carried out aboard HMS *Dreadnought* in September 1907.

▲ Held captive in the hand vice.

▲ Applying the gore.

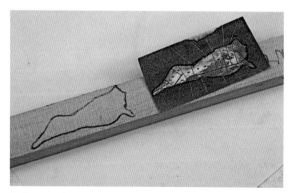

▲ Carving of the beef (pattern).

Carving the Beef

The pattern for my half-carcass of beef came from a recipe book of the sort printed in the mid-1960s, showing cuts of meat for the housewife or cook to recognise at the butcher's shop. The scaled outline was transferred onto a small piece of jelutong timber, which

▲ Suspended from the embarking davit.

in its natural state is the colour of bone. A half-carcass, with the rib cage and backbone showing, is a much more interesting shape than an unbutchered animal.

The carving of this sort of item in miniature is not difficult, provided that you can secure the shape firmly. I use something called a universal work holder, which was originally designed as an engraver's tool. The pin arrangement can be modified to suit practically any shape of work, with the knob acting as an adjustable tensioning device. It is technically known as a vice. The internal carving was done with a 2mm spoon gouge, cleaned up on the end grain with a dental burr.

Realising that the colouring of this sort of item requires more subtlety than enamel paints can deliver, I first of all sealed the item with a coat of aliphatic glue, and when that had dried, finished the more gory paintwork with watercolours red to brown, and a surprising amount of dark blue in the cavities and extremities. The bone structure is just the jelutong with nothing else added. The water colours were then sealed with two coats of a satin spray, in order to give it a slight sheen and seal in the pigment.

The whole exercise is a reminder that fighting ships of all nations had to be regularly supplied with meat as a vital source of energy, and that the quality of the food was often reflected in the morale of the ship's company. It was difficult to provide variety, but monotony and poor quality could quickly lead to the breakdown of discipline and, in extreme cases, mutiny. In the British Navy the general mess system slowly gave way to canteens, and the ending of rations as the responsibility of crew members to share out amongst themselves.

A Boatbuilder's Tale

To finish this section on a historical note as well as a nautical one, I offer the following extraordinary coincidence about *Thunderer*'s 42ft sailing launch.

Edward Hannaford is one of those men who has lived to be a quiet legend in his own lifetime. He has worked, man and boy, in the fishing village of Salcombe, Devon, in the United Kingdom, building and repairing boats. He served his apprenticeship on the site of a boatyard which once produced the most beautiful fruit schooners the world has ever seen. On hearing four years ago that I was embarking on a model of HMS *Thunderer* (1911), he chanced the remark that up until 1963, or thereabouts, Salcombe harbour had had a 42ft naval cutter named *Thunderer*. She was used for general harbour duties, including work associated with the four-masted barque *Herzogin Cecile*, towed into nearby Starehole Bay in 1936 as a partial wreck.

'The remarkable thing about this cutter,' and here Edward Hannaford paused for a moment, 'was that she was, I believe, the first naval cutter to be fitted with an internal combustion engine.' I have no reason to doubt this statement, given that the Thames Iron Works had been making their own engines for cars and lorries for at least four years prior to 1911, and logic would dictate that an internal combustion engine would support the call for speed over tradition with such a large auxiliary boat. If the story is true, and seems plausible, it means that this boat played a part in both the First and Second World Wars. Salcombe harbour was a centre for the preparations for the D-Day landings on 6 June 1944, with many landing craft hidden away under the leafy cover of East Portlemouth on the other side of the estuary. A joint British and American amphibious force sailed from Salcombe on 4 June 1944 to take part in the great Allied landings in Normandy. The concrete launching ramp leading out of the woods to get these craft into the water has only recently been dismantled. The evidence is convincing enough for me to have carried out the necessary addition of an internal combustion engine at the stern of the cutter, and converting the rudder and propeller housing on the underside of the hull, whilst retaining the overall shape of the vessel.

▲ Edward Hannaford. Photo: David Multon LRPS.

▲ The 42ft naval cutter is seen alongside the doomed
windjammer, abreast of the mainmast of the sinking wreck. Source:
Malcom Darch library collection.

▼ 'Those magnificent men in their flying machines!' – the Short
Bros 184 Dover-type floatplane at full throttle.
Photo: Josh Mowll.

Folding Wings and Floatplanes

The Wright brothers' first tentative demonstration of
controlled powered flight using a fixed wing aircraft at
Kitty Hawk, North Carolina, on 17 December 1903
unleashed the future of powered flight on an unready
world. This new development was not initially seen in
the context of planes being used in any theatre of war,
as the mere fact of keeping planes in the air was
challenge enough, but it would be barely six years
before the formation of the first embryonic Naval
Squadron in 1909, on the Isle of Sheppey in Kent, in
the UK. This stunning rate of progress continued, and
by 1911 pilots were flying these flimsy constructions,
not only from prepared flying grounds, but also from
cliff tops, ramps, platforms and in the latter part of the
First World War, from ship's gun turrets with wooden
flying-off ramps facing into the wind. The very first
flight from a moving ship was achieved on 2 May 1912,
from the 1905 pre-dreadnought battleship, *Hibernia*,
on a ramp which ran from the wheelhouse to the
jackstaff. The plane is remarkably similar to the Wright
brothers' original design, but built by Shorts as a
modified S27 pusher biplane.

It is not generally known that, in 1909, Wilbur and

Orville Wright struck a deal in the UK by granting a
licence to the Hon Charles S Rolls, the car manufacturer, to have 'Wright Flyers' built in England, and Eustace
and Oswald Short, joined by their brother Horace,
quickly organised a new factory to build these and
other machines at Shellness, on the Isle of Sheppey,
overlooking the Swale estuary. It was Horace Short who
designed the folding-wing, torpedo-carrying 184
floatplane, a brilliant concept in flexible storage which
continued in naval seaplane design from that day to
this. The remains of this first British aircraft factory are
still there and one hopes that they will one day be
restored.

The Royal Naval Air Service

The story of the Royal Naval Air Service (RNAS) began on the Isle of Sheppey. The government of the day, under the Liberal Party of Lord Asquith (1852-1928) had largely come down on the side of balloons and dirigibles in terms of provision for air cover on both land and sea. In government circles the role of aircraft in future warfare was largely dismissed as a serious concern, and the development costs associated with the nascent aircraft industry were therefore left in civilian hands.

The Short brothers were more long-sighted than the War Office, and the factory building the new planes in the run up to the First World War was so industrious and successful that they were in the unique position of being able to offer the Royal Navy aeroplanes and floatplanes for training officers in the art of flying from land and water. It was not long before the RNAS established at Eastchurch (Sheppey) on the Kent coast, and had their own Squadron of eight planes – and a truly odd selection they were.

During the war years, the RNAS developed into both a shore-based as well as a seagoing operation. Floatplanes had to be transported in civilian ships, converted from their peacetime service, which were capable of keeping pace with the Grand Fleet. The most famous of these seaplane tenders was *Engadine*, a cross-channel packet boat from which Flight Lt Frederick J Rutland flew his famous reconnaissance mission on the orders of Admiral David Beatty, just prior to the battle of Jutland. Rutland, in his Short 184 No. 8359, spotted from the low cloud ceiling of 900ft four German light cruisers, which opened fire on him but failed to hit the seaplane. Beatty was to write later that the sighting 'did indicate that seaplanes under such circumstances are of distinct value.' The remains of the forward fuselage of 8359 are preserved in an unrestored state at the Fleet Air Arm Museum at Yeovilton, UK.

As the war progressed in 1917, one of the main duties of the RNAS was to aid in the battle against the U-boat. The RNAS employed both seaplanes and non-rigid airships to carry out reconnaissance work. Although the airships were slower, they were more easily able to carry effective wireless transmitters aloft, which were too heavy for all but the most powerful seaplanes. The very presence of the larger seaplanes meant that U-boats were forced to travel below the surface of the water, and the majority of the larger seaplanes carried bombs in racks when not armed with an expensive torpedo.

Turret Ramps

There is no photographic evidence that *Thunderer* ever carried her own aircraft, but the naval historian, Oscar Parkes, and others, record that she was one of the first to have flying-off ramps fitted to her two super-firing turrets B and X in 1917. There is a picture postcard which clearly shows that these ramps existed, clamped down on the barrels of the 13 1/2in guns. These folding platforms were large structures, 62ft long, which interfered with the normal operation of the super-firing turrets but, despite their size and length, they could only be used by small scout planes, some fitted with skids, some with wheeled dollies, and mostly 2F-1s with standard undercarriages.

The downside of this new innovation with scouting planes was the necessary ditching and recovery at the end of the flight, for which these land planes were ill-equipped. For the intrepid pilots, there was no guarantee of being retrieved before the flying machine, despite flotation bags, had started to sink. The vessels picking up the pilots would often not be those from which the plane was originally launched, and this added a further dimension to the pilot's concern for being fished out of the water. At this point, one needs to be reminded that these planes were being flown by cavalry officers, men who were used to the idea of horses blindly jumping over walls, not knowing what might lie on the other side. It was said by the then Lord Grosvenor that he considered the aeroplane to be 'a military development of the horse.' Admiral David Beatty was also of this breed. In peacetime, he loved to ride to hounds and conducted his naval engagements with the same kind of bravado.

▲ Close-up of the forward flying off ramp, fitted to 'B' turret on *Thunderer* in 1917. There appears to be some kind of cradle or dolly at the top of the ramp, and a break in the runway to allow for the elevation of the gun barrels. Photo taken in 1921 by Gieves Ltd from a collection owned by John Hamlin.

The Flying-Off Ramp in Miniature

Whether or not there were ever Admiralty drawings for the construction of these ramps, I cannot say. There does not seem to be uniformity in the pictures of them which I have come across, and they do all share a slightly spatchcocked look. I am also faced with the issue that the model ones need to be easily removable, so the ramp must be made with that in mind.

It is basically a simple piece of table-sawing, of the type which in full scale could be easily knocked up in the carpenter's shop, aided and abetted by the blacksmith. The original ramps were capable of being hinged back, so that the gun turret could be used for its normal purpose. Upside down, the ramp looks uncannily like wooden railway track, with four upright crutches to hold it in place. The crutches are made from hammered brass tube, which gives a bit of spring to the metal and just the right amount of grip. The metal crutches have been leathered for extra grip, and also because they would otherwise damage the barrels. In the old days of wooden sail, all the yokes of booms were similarly treated with leather in their jaws to protect the masts from being chafed.

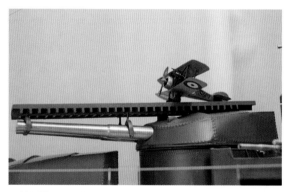

▲ N6182 on the flying-off ramp. Note the Lewis gun through the upper wing section.

▲ The underside of the flying-off ramp.

Manufacture in Miniature of the Short 184 (Improved) Dover Type

I wanted to tackle what I regarded as the most difficult challenge first, and over the past few months I had been gazing at all sorts of images of early aircraft. The smaller biplanes already mentioned appear sporty and experimental. The larger wingspan required by the more powerful floatplanes, which were able to land and take off from the water, and carry a greater payload, appear burdened under their own weight when at rest. In flight, pictures show them soaring like eagles, and one can easily associate, in a surrogate and vicarious way, with the thrill and the complexity of keeping one of these huge machines in level flight, to say nothing of the sheer physical stamina it took to fly them off the water, and keep them airborne. Landing them must have been a challenge of nerves and concentration. No wonder these pilots were regarded as daredevils with 'but a short time to live.'

The one focal point which all these early aircraft have in common is the bird. Horace Short's design with the 184 machine even has a display of feathering at the wing tips, imitating what he had observed from nature, and replicating it on the trailing edge of the wing flaps. He had visited the Antarctic and was particularly impressed by the flight of the albatross.

Thetford's *British Naval Aircraft 1912-58* (1958) provides the technical data for the Short 184, which are as follows:

- Description: two-seat reconnaissance, bombing and torpedo-carrying seaplane with foldback wings; wooden structure, fabric-covered.
- Manufacturers: Short Bros, Kent; there were a total of nine other subcontractors.
- Power plant: in the case of the one being modelled (Short 184 Dover type N1098), the engine was a Sunbeam Maori developing 260hp. This engine was fitted to late production models.
- Dimensions: span 63ft 6in; length 40ft 7in; height 13ft 6in.
- Cooling radiator: flat frontal car type, replacing the mounted Samovar box radiator of earlier models, which obscured the pilot's view (the Samovar was a Russian tea urn which provided a constant source of hot water!).
- Weight: empty 3,703lb; loaded 5,363lb; fully-armed 2.62 tons.
- Performance: maximum speed 88.5mph at 2,000ft; 84mph at 6,500ft.

- Climb: 8min 35sec to 2,000ft; 33min 50sec to 6,500ft.
- Endurance: 2h 45min.
- Service ceiling: 9,000ft.
- Armaments: provision for one free-mounted Lewis machine gun aft, and one 14in torpedo (weight 810lb) or various loads of bombs up to a maximum of 520lb.

Built-in Lightness

The problem with producing a model which is light and delicate, at the same time as being robust enough to construct and handle, is a challenging one. It is my opinion that the smaller the object to be modelled becomes, the more the modeller must face up to metal fabrication. The inherent strength of metal, even a soft metal like copper, when it is worked and thereby hardened, gives a crispness and definition which timber, despite all its virtues and versatility, cannot.

From many hours of making the plating lines on the hull, I had noticed how working with copper sheet using hammers and forming tools gives this metal real rigidity. Corrugation reinforces this, and it occurred to me that if the wings were formed with a ribbed pattern worked into them, they would be strong enough to withstand soldering the upper and lower wing sections together, and also retain the apparent lightness of construction so essential for realism.

▲ Wing former section.

▲ Milling out the rib formers.

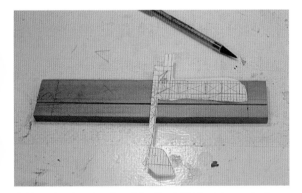

▲ Measuring the wing ribs of the Short 184 floatplane onto the boxwood former.

▲ Preparing the curvature of the wing section.

▲ Softening the grooves with a round-faced needle file.

Wing Construction

Boxwood is once again the timber of choice for making the former for the wing surface and curvature, combining this with milled corrugations. It is basically a comb into which it is possible to work the copper sheet by running a form tool into the grooved slot. I used the backside of a 90-degree scriber for this, because the diminishing diameter of the spike allows for indentation depth and definition. The process is the same as brass rubbing, or shading in the image of a coin with pencil and paper, but the effect is to strengthen greatly the copper shim, aided by a run of an impressing tool around the edge of the wing. The curvature of the upper wing is slightly emphasised by use of a wooden handle, in this case using the opposite end of the impressing tool, and running the wooden handle along the surface a few times. The leading edge of the wing has a wooden supporting spar on the underside in order to keep some rigidity to the structure. The pilot and observer's cockpit are not simply round holes, so it requires a miller bit to elongate them into the correct shape. Boxwood was used for the fuselage because it carves and models so well, leaving a crisp edge to the work.

▼ Copper sheet is overlaid on the former and the first rib structure is impressed with the metal scriber.

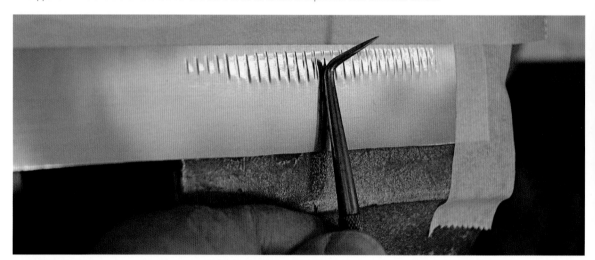

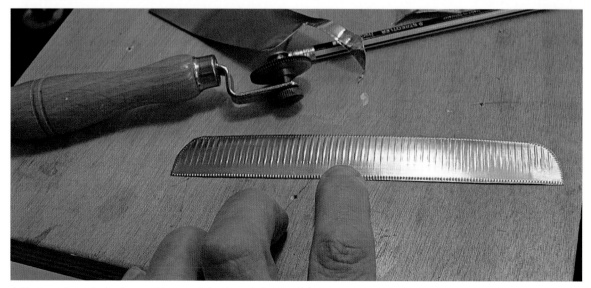

▲ First experimental wing (not used, but proof that the technique works).

Centre of Gravity

The Short Bros 184 design can be seen in different configurations from a study of the many versions and experiments which were taking place at the time. The plan I followed comes from *Jane's All the World's Aircraft 1919* (1969 reprint), and shows the two cockpits close together, the pilot being largely hidden under the upper wing section. Some other photos show the position slightly further aft, but the critical factor here is the point of balance on the wings of the plane. There is one picture of an observer climbing from the forward cockpit to the aft position in order to distribute his body weight after take-off, which underlines how critical this tipping point on the centre of gravity was to the balance of the plane in flight.

On the model the wings are soldered together which, in photographic terms, looks like a bit of overkill. This method does, however, give the full wingspan a great deal of added strength. Gripping hold of any delicate structure like this is a problem, and only solder is strong enough to withstand what happens next. A chainsaw sharpener is used to feather the edge of the wing tips and show the tail feathers. On the prototype these would presumably have acted as air-

brakes, as well as preventing stalling tendencies at low speeds. Maun pliers, with their parallel grip action set in the grip of the vice, gave me the chance to carry out the grinding task successfully, one which presents a potentially destructive vibrating motion to so fragile a piece.

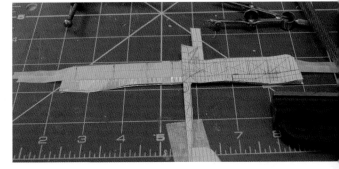

▲ Half pattern of the 184 wing section, laid over both the upper and lower wings.

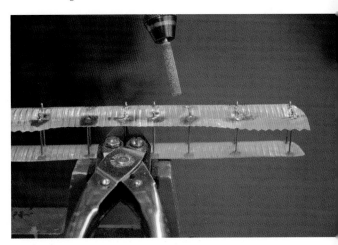

▲ Soft-soldering the upper and lower wings.

Rigging

No wing section of this period is complete without the rigging of the tensioning wires. On the model these are made from drawn brass wire, which is the way to produce a rigid-looking wire in very thin section. The wire is stretched literally almost to breaking point, and being brass takes well to being soldered into position, particularly if it is first 'tinned' at the point of contact. This procedure once again strengthens the wing section and, even in miniature, begins to have the essence of one of the 'early birds' of flight. The model makes no attempt slavishly to include all the rigging and control lines; there comes a point where such attentions on so

▲ Milling out the cockpits for the pilot and observer.

▲ Wire cross bracing.

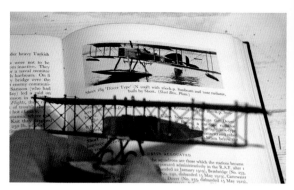

▲ Image of the emerging model of the Dover Type N1098.

small a scale become pointlessly complicated and over-delicate. I imagine that this plane will be 'flown' by generations of children and grandchildren; it is therefore more important that it should be made with a structural robustness in mind, although there are very vulnerable parts which could be damaged quite easily.

The Floats

These were made from boxwood on the model, with struts fabricated from brass tube hammered flat. This technique gives strength and flexibility, both of which are required for an undercarriage. They are soldered on the model to a small brass platform, in recognition that

fitting them directly to the fuselage would be likely to fail after a few landings. The originals followed a very simple design made from timber, with a form which tried to dispense with what is known as 'stick'. This describes the surface tension of smooth water clinging to the skim of the floats, stopping the aircraft from lifting away. Pilots preferred weather conditions with a small amount of disturbance to the surface water rather than a totally smooth stretch. Such conditions tested these under-powered and over-laden machines to the utmost, straining every sinew to become airborne.

Aircraft Propellers

Aircraft propellers are a fascinating subject which deserve a great deal more attention and knowledge than I possess, but the principles for all propellers remain much the same. It is the combination of an indexing machine and a milling machine table being used together for the

▲ The floats and undercarriage.

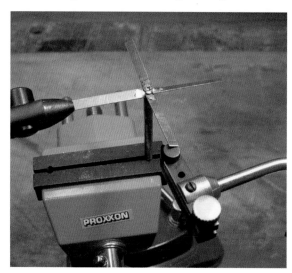

▲ The four-bladed propeller set up for soldering.

manufacture of the hub which makes this task relatively simple and accurate. With four slots set at 90 degrees to one another, and a set of 20 degrees at the root of the blade, the machined groove made by the dental router bit allows for fixing the blades in the right relationship to one another, aided by some improvised variable clamps. The propeller is then sweated in soft-solder to the centre hub of the prop. The strange-looking clamps are from the world of fly-fishing, for those who like to tie their own flies for trout and salmon.

Wrong Again

All went well with this procedure until I read that the Maori Sunbeam engine fitted to the Dovers had left-handed propellers, and you will see that my first attempt is right-handed. All the Renault engines were fitted with right-handers, so I had to do it all again, facing the indexer towards the opposite hand. This time I was also more mindful of the propeller blades' leading edge, which has a sharp but rounded form, like a scimitar blade, so that the exercise in having to remake the second one turned out to be a good piece of discipline, and I also now have a spare French one. A useful tip when making propellers is to leave a long

▲ Linishing off the blades of the first (French) propeller.

piece of rod on the aft side, which can be put back in the lathe, or any drill chuck, for trimming and truing up. The strap linisher is also invaluable for grinding the shape of the blades. Because the four-bladed propeller is made of brass, it spins satisfactorily by blowing on it. Continual motion for photographic purposes can be provided by a small hairdryer.

▼ Unfinished model perched on X-turret with the wrong (French) propeller fitted. (There is no suggestion that a Short 184 floatplane could take off from a gun turret).

Livery

After a spray undercoat of matt grey, a livery in what might be described as the colour of midnight was applied. This night camouflage was of a type adopted by the RNAS, and requires the roundels of the decals to be edged, and the lettering, along with the underside of the wings and fuselage, to be off-white. Then it all needs to be quietened down with a covering of French button-polish, including the lettering and the decals, giving it that oily, used look. The lettering and the decals are by the company of BECC in self-adhesive vinyl.

In reality, the photographic session which made N1098 famous was undertaken at Queenborough in June 1917, showing the floatplane's neat car bonnet hinged cowling and frontal-honeycombed radiator. The vents on the bonnet are unbelievably crude, the result perhaps of the pilot's bitter complaint that the new style radiator was prone to overheating whilst taxiing before take-off. One can imagine the orders given to 'do something about it', resulting in the crude finish to the grilles. It is the only example I have spotted with forward rake to the exhaust system, and a single pipe on the starboard side connected to the engine's manifold. This was obviously under conversion, because by July 1917 the exhaust manifold is vented from the front of the engine, and the pipe raked aft. By September of that year the plane was at Yarmouth, and ultimately deleted about a year later. At the time of writing, I am so confused about this plane's 'improved history' that I have not decided which end the exhaust pipe should go.

A small stowing cradle was constructed, just to anchor this plane to Q-turret. It may look like a take-off ramp, but this plane could only take off by first being lowered into the water from the ship's crane, attached to the stump pole.

The Two Camels

It is difficult not to fall in love with the Camel, despite its diminutive size. As a backyard dreamer it is not impossible to consider building one's own in full scale. With the fuselage at just over 18ft in length, it is actually no longer than the length of a standard saloon car.

There are two versions of the Camel: the F-1, which was nicknamed the 'camel' because of the twin humps into which the two synchronised Vickers machine guns were housed, and a naval version called the 2F-l. The original Camels were supplied to both the Royal Flying Corps (RFC) and the RNAS, and quickly gained a reputation as wonderful flying machines with both the Army and the Navy. Their many exploits on the Western Front have been well chronicled.

In 1917, the prototype shipboard version of the fighter was tested in March and introduced in May, superseding and replacing the Sopwith Pups. The Sopwith 2F-1 had the advantage that the tail was

▼ Plan of the F1 Camel. Source: *Jane's All the World's Aircraft, 1919* (1969 reprint).

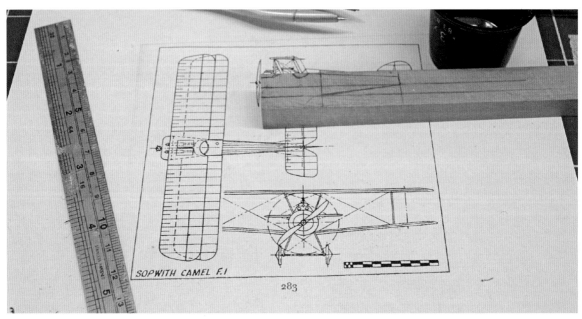

SOPWITH CAMEL F.1

283

detachable for easier stowage aboard ship, and there was provision made for a mounted Lewis gun on the upper wing, to pair up with a single synchronised Vickers gun, placed dead ahead of the pilot on the port side only. The Lewis gun mounted on the top wing was for raking fire at kite balloons and Zeppelins. The naval version was thirteen inches less in wingspan, and the vast majority of them ended up being fitted with the Bentley BR1 as their standard power plant. This engine was more powerful at 150hp and more reliable than the Clerget engine fitted to the F-1s, although there were still problems being experienced with differential cooling on the cylinders: cool at the front and hot at the back is not good for an aluminium engine. According to Bruce Robertson in *Sopwith – The Man and His Aircraft* (1970), the contract price of a Camel airframe without guns or instruments was £874.10s. The Bentley Rotary Engine (BR1) added a further £650 to the total.

Sopwith Camel 2F-1: The Shipboard Fighter

By October 1918 there were 129 Camel 2F-ls in service, and 112 were carried in ships of the Grand Fleet. One of the many intended roles for the 2F-1 planes was to destroy Zeppelins flying over the North Sea. These new planes served on four carriers, ten battleships and seventeen cruisers during the First World War, and by 1918 they were also flown from aircraft carriers and from lighters towed by destroyers. The first successful take-off by this makeshift method was achieved by Flight Sub-Lieutenant Stuart D Cully on 31 July 1918. A few days afterwards on the 10 August, Cully shot down Zeppelin L53 whilst flying from a towed lighter – this was the last Zeppelin to be destroyed during combat. Sopwith aircraft N6812 is the only surviving 2F-l in this country, and is preserved at London's Imperial War Museum. The plane was ditched in the sea after its major triumph, but both pilot and plane were recovered by the attendant lighter, and the plane was presented at the end of the war to the Imperial War Museum for permanent display. This is the one I have chosen to model. Whether or not she ever flew from *Thunderer*'s ramps is up for conjecture, but the likelihood is that other similar aircraft would have done. The story of this plane's survival is that it was stored on the east coast after the First World War, and also exhibited at the Schoolboy's Own Exhibition in 1933-4. Another original surviving 2F-1 (N8156) is in the Canadian War Museum.

Construction of 2F-1 in Miniature

Following on from the experience of making the model Short 184, the wings and the tailplane were constructed off the plan, using the same ribbed former for the copper wings. The profiling of the leading and trailing edges was achieved by the repoussé technique of a dry ballpoint being used to impress around the edge seam from the reverse side of the metal. Into the leading edge only, as with the 184 plane, a length of strengthening brass wire was soft-soldered to the top and bottom wing, just to give the copper sheet some lateral rigidity.

▲ The fuselage, wings and tailplane are united.

The Fuselage

I knew from the outset that the fuselage and engine housing were going to have to be centred into the four-jaw independent chuck, in order to reproduce accurately the circular cowling at the nose of the airframe. Boxwood, the pattern maker's dream timber, was used once again: it machines in a lathe almost as well as metal. The cowling is brass tube, nosed in with a rounded steel punch tool, clamped in the tool holder, with the lathe running. This technique is well known to metal spinners, and it can be done with flaring out as well as pushing in, and is best carried out with annealed (previously heated) metal, and a little candle wax to ease the contact with the spinning metal.

Only the original F-1 can truly claim to be a Camel, with its twin-mounted armament either side of the fairing hump, but the naval version hung onto the nickname, despite having only one Vickers machine gun placed directly forward of the pilot on the portside.

On the model, the addition of the undercarriage and wheels turns this small plane into the beauty she has always been. The iconic shape of the straight upper wing matched with the dihedral of the lower wings raked back is an unmistakable winner. This was a design not only pleasing on the eye, but a configuration that would have an influence on a whole generation of planes to follow.

Although the plane had a wonderful reputation with pilots for manoeuvrability, it was not an aircraft for novices or the inexperienced. The gyroscopic effect of the powerful engine on a very small airframe accounted for its dog-fighting reputation, but it also took some taming and mastering before man and machine became as one.

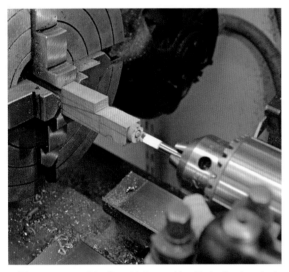

▲ The nose cone of the Camel being machined in the four-jaw chuck.

▲ Close-up of the nose cone. Note the dihedral on the lower wing section. The starboard Vicker's machine gun, shown here, was later replaced by a Lewis gun, pointing upwards through the upper wing section to facilitate raking fire.

▲ The Bentley-Rolls BR1. Picture taken at Air and Space Museum, Washington, DC.

The Synchronisation of Gunfire

This gun was provided with what I think is one of the most incredible feats of engineering, the Constaninesco synchronisation gear which, by using impulses transmitted from a column of liquid instead of the earlier mechanical linkages, enabled the pilot to fire machine guns through a high revving propeller without shooting away the wooden blades. By mid-1917 the new CC gear provided the pilot with a rate of fire similar to that of a standard machine gun.

Technical Data for F-1 and 2F-1 Camel

- Description: single seat shipboard fighting scout. Wooden structure, fabric covered.
- Manufacturers: William Beardmore & Co Ltd, Dalmuir, Dumbartonshire.
- Power Plant: 150hp Bentley BR1.
- Dimensions: span 26ft 11in; length 18ft 8in; height 9ft 1in.
- Weights with BR1 engine: empty 1,036lb; loaded 1,530lb.
- Performance with BR1: maximum speed 124mph at 6,500ft.
- Climb: 25 minutes to 15,000ft.
- Service ceiling: 17,300ft.
- Armament: one fixed, synchronised Vickers machine gun; one Lewis gun above the wing centre section; provision for two 50lb bombs in racks below the wings.

Source: Owen Thetford, *British Naval Aircraft 1912-1958* (1958).

▲ Both aircraft on the deck showing the difference in size.

Side by side, the Short 184 and the 2F-1 together admirably demonstrate their differing roles in the emergent world of ships and planes together post-Jutland, the scout plane and the bomber/submarine hunter. They also demonstrate how much bigger a plane has to be if it is going to carry a torpedo or a radio transmitter, rather than just acting as a scout or recon-naissance fighter plane.

Finishing the Model

Finishing a model after five years of study and practical work is a hesitant moment. Every modelmaker, of whatever level of skill, knows that he or she could have done more, so that knowing when to stop turns out to be a matter of experience. Oil painters and water-colourists suffer from the same set of variables. It is perfectly possible to spoil a picture or a model by doing too much.

I am keen that matters of seamanship make sense, and that details such as ladders would allow crew members to move from one level of the ship to another. Rigging, both static and running, is another area which would cause an expert eye to be raised were this to be a strictly static model in a glass case, because only a minimal amount of these lines are present. No funnel

stays for instance, and no fore and aft braces to the main yard. As mentioned in the text, this is because of access to the working parts, and their omission is the compromise which has to be paid for ready access by human hands.

As to the model itself, I hope it has somehow captured the dark menace of a twentieth-century battleship, and I also trust that it looks like an object which has been fabricated using the old production methods of hammer and rivet, of casting in heavy metal and fire welding. I do like a ship model to look as though it was made in a shipyard which acknowledges and embraces engineering as well as shipwrighting. The full title of the Thames Iron Works in its later life had the addition of the words 'Shipbuilding and Engineering Co Ltd', and I have tried hard to salute that aspect of the works.

I remain astonished that human hands constructed these battleships, and that these vessels were expected to work, on the high seas, in all seasons and in all weathers, twenty-four hours a day, and also provide a home for 738 loyal officers and men. That is what really impresses me, and that is the lasting legacy from that generation one hundred years ago to the present day.

The completed model.

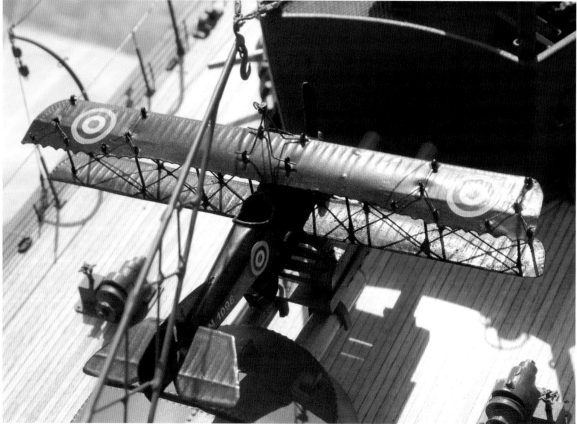

CHAPTER 8

～ *HMS* Thunderer and *USS* Texas ～

The USS *Texas*

Serendipity has played a bit part in my life: the word is described in the dictionary as 'making a happy and unexpected discovery by accident.' And quite serendipitously, I found a book which was, rather unfairly in my opinion, on the remaindered book stall of a shop in the university city of Cambridge. The book was *The Battleships* (2000) by Rob McCauley and Ian Johnston, published as a tie-in to a Channel 4 film, and the authors draw attention to the fact that there is still one battleship left in the world from the 1912 period with a profile and specification which bear a marked similarity to those of HMS *Thunderer*. That battleship is USS *Texas*. The similarities are striking:

The Visit

At the time I first read about the existence of this ship, there was no way in which I could have considered a visit to St Jacinto Park in Texas, but recent retirement allowed me to entertain a hazy notion that here was a ship I simply had to see with my own eyes before finishing the model. My two previous books, on the SS *Great Britain* (1843) and HMS *Warrior* (1860), had allowed me to explore fully both these preserved vessels, and breathe in their life force, before making large models of them. With the current model, this had simply not been possible, because *Thunderer* was broken up years ago and nothing recognisable is left. I genuinely began to realise that there had been an enormous emotional gap in this regard, which had not

Comparison of HMS *Thunderer* and USS *Texas*		
	HMS *Thunderer*	USS *Texas*
Ordered	23 January 1910	24 June 1910
Keel laid	13 April 1910	17 April 1911
Launched	1 Feb 1911	18 May 1912
Commissioned	May 1912	March 1914
Length	581ft	573ft
Beam	88ft	95.2ft
Draught	24ft	29.5ft
Displacement	22,500	27,000
Propulsion	Turbines (4)	Triple expansion (2)
Speed	20.7 knots	21 knots
Main Armament	110 x 13 1/2in	10 x 14in
Secondary	16 x 4in	21 x 5in

In short, *Thunderer* was slightly longer and slimmer in the waist, but *Texas* was more heavily armed and marginally faster. Despite the fact that they were built so many miles apart, they are virtually the same age and have a very similar build, with all their big guns on the centre line, first established by the American designers, and copied by the British.

existed with my other two projects. In short, I needed to go and embrace some early twentieth-century armour plate, and if it was on the other side of the world, then so be it.

Nothing really prepares you for the sight of a full-sized battleship. There is a smouldering menace about these vessels that is not conveyed by the camera, or any other medium. You simply have to go and experience for yourself the feeling of hostile intent and impending catastrophe which an engine of war like this brings. There is no substitute in this world which allows you to receive the full impact of these war machines, other than gazing in awe and wonder at their length and their breadth and their height. It slowly dawns on you that this is a machine designed to kill people when all other possibilities for negotiation have broken down. It is the result of the abject and obvious failure of human beings to live in peace and harmony with one another, material evidence of the steps mankind is prepared to take when defensive measures fail, and brutish force remains the only option.

In the same instant, there dawns the realisation that

▼ The jackstaff, USS *Texas*, 11 November 2008.

a fighting ship is also a home, a place where men live, and move, and have their being. They have to eat and work and mess together, as well as carry out their specific duties. This is a place of discipline, where order and training is put into practice, and practice makes perfect. It is a place where men give of their entire selves in the cause of freedom and justice and patriotism.

History and Place

It so happened that our first day's visit to the ship coincided with what in Britain is called Armistice Day, and in America is called Veterans' Day, and at the 11th hour of the 11th day of the 11th month of 2008 we were able to stand on the fo'c'sle deck, beside the mighty guns, for a minute's silence and contemplate the honourable service of this ship in both world wars,

FIRST MARINE DIVISION
WAS
FOUNDED ABOARD USS TEXAS (BB 35)
WHEN A DIRECTIVE WAS READ ON THE SHIP'S
FANTAIL REDESIGNATING 1st MARINE BRIGADE ON
1 FEBRUARY 1941
WHILE THE BATTLESHIP WAS FLAGSHIP FOR
CARIBBEAN AMPHIBIOUS EXERCISES.
RENOWNED FOR VALOR IN BATTLE FROM ITS LEGENDARY ACTION AT GUADALCANAL
THROUGH THE ARDUOUS PACIFIC CAMPAIGNS OF WORLD WAR II,
FIRST MARINE DIVISION ESTABLISHED A TRADITION OF COURAGE AND TENACITY
SUSTAINED THROUGH COMBAT IN KOREA, VIETNAM AND SUBSEQUENT CONFLICTS.

"SEMPER FIDELIS!"
THIS PLAQUE IS PRESENTED TO THE BATTLESHIP TEXAS
THIS 1st DAY OF FEBRUARY 1991
BY THE FIRST MARINE DIVISION ASSOCIATION
IN HONOR OF HER HISTORICAL PARTICIPATION
IN THE BIRTH OF THE FIRST MARINE DIVISION

those who served on her in the early years, and those who were there at the Normandy beaches and later at Iwo Jima. The only sound was the fluttering of the United States Union Jack, the starred blue canton without the stripes, which on a US Navy vessel stands alone as a maritime flag at the prow of the ship. This ship has a special historical connection with the US

▲ First Marine Division plaque.

Marines, in that the First Marine Division was founded aboard USS *Texas* on 1 February 1941, when the battleship was also the flagship for the Caribbean

▼ View of the ship from the Battleground Monument.

▲ Engine feed pump rev counter.

Amphibious Exercises, and there is a bronze plaque aboard commemorating this, presented by the First Marine Division Association.

The ship lies at anchor in St Jacinto Park, which is where in April 1836 the State of Texas won its independence from Mexico. Six weeks previously the famous battle of the Alamo had taken place, where the Texans were routed by the Mexicans at St Antonio. At St Jacinto battleground, the outcome was reversed, but once again, with great loss of life and intense hand-to-hand fighting. From the top of the famous nearby pyramid monument to this battle, it is possible to see the extent of both the wet lands and the oil refineries which surround her berth. The stone monument and the battleship are of equivalent height and length at 570ft, not including the lone star of Texas which adds another 34ft to its stature.

The ship herself has a fascinating history, arising initially out of American awareness that European instability required the United States to arm herself in order to protect her own shores against imperialist powers. I was surprised to learn that in 1906 it was not Germany who was second largest naval power after Great Britain, but the United States. There was only one sister ship built, namely USS *New York*, laid down on 11 September 1911, and launched on 30 October 1912, designated BB34. She was built at the Brooklyn Naval Yard, New York City. The USS *Texas* BB35 was built further south at the Newport News Shipbuilding & Dry Dock Co; imagine my personal delight in finding the engraved evidence of this in existence on the revolution counter of the feed pump in the engine room, frozen in time on 014221.

The Reciprocating Engines

The engine room of *Texas* is currently only partly restored, which to me, perversely, is a delight. The team on the ship are very properly making every effort to stop the ravages of rust, but the task is enormous, on top of the everyday jobs to which attention must be given. There is an added problem of humidity: the atmosphere is wet and sticky, and the ship sweats on the inside when it is hot, and on the outside when it is not. The temperature in midsummer soars to over 50°C, and requires air conditioning in the inhabited parts of the vessel, but there are pockets of the ship where this simply is not possible or practical to implement. Even in November, the fans are running at full blast.

▲ Con-rod and cross-head of main portside engine.

▲ Thrust block oilers, USS *Texas*.

▼ Thrust bearing being machined at the former John Penn's Engineering Works, Greenwich, London.

The Americans chose to engine USS *Texas* with reciprocating, rather than turbine, engines, for the reason that they had experienced difficulties with turbine manufacture in reaching the specifications required by the US Navy Board. Turbines were also not quite as flexible in operation as the more familiar triple expansion steam engines, which had a good record of reliability, shared with a rather noisy reputation. There was also the simplification on this ship of only two propellers and a single rudder of pre-dreadnought design.

Below decks it was a difficult task to photograph the unlit engine room, but glimpses of the big and small ends of the con-rods hint at the size of this gargantuan monster, which was the twinned heartbeat of the vessel. Even the power-assisted steering gear is a study in practical heavy engineering.

The thrust bearing was of particular interest to me, in that I had the old photograph taken of the machine shop at John Penn's works engaged in exactly that manufacturing task. To see such a thing installed, with all its oilers in place, and the flipped-over cap of the oil bath/reservoir, tied a mental knot for me across the Atlantic, and across time itself, forcing me to consider the question of who was really responsible for the development of the super-dreadnought. Who was there first? Who exactly was responsible for all the parts that made these ships work, the sum of the parts making the whole? I think the answer to these important rhetorical questions lie in the enormous detail which these vessels carried. Everywhere you look, the component parts come from different places, and have slightly differing designs and configurations, yet when they are all joined together and coupled up, they contribute to something called 'the fighting ship.'

When later I visited the Johnson Space Centre in Houston, and saw mock-ups of the latest International Space Station, the same thought recurred. The contribution to the whole unit is the result of worldwide experiment on the very edge of what man can achieve scientifically. No battleship design can be attributed to any one nation, because new ideas themselves know no boundaries.

1918 – Joined in Service

The two sisters USS *Texas* and USS *New York* joined the British Grand Fleet after Jutland, in December 1917, constituting the Sixth Battle Squadron at Scapa Flow, known to Americans as Division Nine. The two fleet divisions did, in fact, sail together. *Texas* first arrived at Scapa Flow on 11 February 1918, and, as well as supporting the Fourth Battle Squadron, escorted convoy missions operating in the North Sea in March

▼ The Orion Class battleships steaming hard in the Moray Firth with the American Squadron.

and April. She entered the Firth of Forth with her division on 12 April before leaving again on 17 April for three days of escort duty. On 23 April the German High Seas Fleet set off from Jade Bay towards the Norwegian coast, threatening an Allied convoy, and the following day *Texas* again headed out to sea in support of the Second Battle Squadron, but the retreating Germans were not spotted until it was too late to engage in battle. Seven months later, after escort and blockade missions, both *Thunderer* and *Texas* would form part of the Grand Escort of the German High Seas Fleet from Wilhelmshaven to the Firth of Forth for surrender on 21 November 1918.

The 1925 Overhaul
In the original configuration of *Texas*, two funnels, or stacks, as they are familiarly known, lead up from the fore and aft boiler rooms. This was in the days of her being coal-fired. Today only one funnel remains, following her modernisation in the spring of 1925 to

oil-firing. Her original profile also carried two of the distinctive cage masts, rather than the tripod conversion seen today. The thinking which lay behind the cage masts was that it is more difficult to disable a woven structure than a tubular one. Their very lightly-built, hooped masts must have produced significant windage, however, adding to the inherent instability of the hull. They appear taller than the tripod masts, which would have been good for spotting, but mechanically difficult for attaching other necessary supports like topmasts and signal yards. Although old-fashioned, they are both distinctive and attractive.

The Anti-Torpedo Bulges/Blisters
These were the first items to be pointed out on the tour of the ship, because they are very apparent and are currently giving concern at the water level and below. There is a mere half an inch of steel thickness left, and

▼ Tripod tower, USS *Texas*.

this will probably mean that the vessel will have to come off her own bottom in the future, and be given a dry berth. The blisters were additions in 1925 in respect of greater attention being paid to the vulnerability of these ships to torpedo attack; her armour plating was also reinforced at the same time. I would be unsure as to how this would have affected her seakeeping, but it provided a double skin and, *in extremis*, may well have saved her life. Sadly, the blisters hide the lean and hungry lines of the original hull, and photographs of her dry-docked in 1989 at nearby Galveston emphasise how dumpy and frumpish she is below the waterline.

The Real Thing

Not a lot of this shows above the waterline, apart from what appears as a slight tumblehome. What you do see is a mighty structure dominated by the 14in gun turrets, and the soaring tripod mast. Although the additions of anti-aircraft guns point to the latter days of the ship, she is still of her time, with her central defensive weaponry, the six 5in guns guarding the ship from the casemate. On the first tour, we were shown these, but the main emphasis was quite properly about life aboard ship in the living quarters, concerned with eating, washing, sleeping, laundry, entertainment, punishment, post and communications.

More than a thousand men lived together on this ship, and it is almost impossible to comprehend this fact without having actually experienced it. This is the main reason why these preserved ships are so important to future generations. Although they are now static exhibits, they silently tell us their story and instruct us in a way that no other medium can touch.

In a world where there is so much information available at the press of a button, there is still no substitute whatsoever for experiencing the real thing. It is all in the fine detail, such as the hammock hooks, where those sailors who had neither space in the bunks nor on the floor, were gently rocked to sleep with the motion of the ship, slung in their hammocks, or the scuttle butts where the crew refreshed themselves with drinking water and, where it is said, gossip spread like wildfire. The dentist's chair, and the barber's shop, and the tailor's shop where alterations and repairs to uniforms would be made, all remind us of our common humanity, and the sacrifices which the crew made for peace and for freedom, living together under such conditions.

My second visit was of a different kind. It simply is not possible to take a group of four people into the kinds of area which I wanted to inspect, so I went alone. Travis Davis, assistant curator, should be mentioned at this point in the story, because without him and his torch and his intimate knowledge of the ship, I would not have been able to take the photographs and gather the information to satisfy some personal curiosities. The first place I wanted to visit was the wheelhouse, way aloft in the masting system.

▼ Forward guns and superstructure, USS *Texas*.

The Wheelhouse

The wheelhouse shares the same flat as the chart house, placed aft, and the conservers are fairly certain that this is all original 1914 period. The surrounding walls of the chart house are made of brass, not steel, in order to avoid a magnetic field surrounding the compass which stands outside and abaft the chart house. At this moment, in my mind a distant penny dropped. Was this why *Thunderer*'s wheelhouse and chart house were both made from timber and not steel?

Magnetism

This may sound obscure and far-fetched, but I knew from studying the 1901 research vessel the SS *Discovery*, which took Scott to the Antarctic on his first expedition, that the whole of the central portion of that ship was free of magnetic material. Even the stove was made of cast brass. HMS *Warrior* was also troubled throughout her life by the magnetic field produced by all that wrought iron, her only reliable compass being placed aloft on the mizzen top. Here was the evidence before my very eyes. If the structure is near a compass, make it of wood or brass or any anti-magnetic material.

Commanding View

The view aloft from the wheelhouse is, quite simply, awe-inspiring, with the delightful detail of round scuttles looking down on the two forward turrets, with their barrels pointing directly towards the pyramid monument of St Jacinto. The top strake of the ship is at its most noticeable from this vantage point, whose casemates beneath provide the opportunity for forward fire from the secondary armament, harking back to the first dreadnought design.

Inside the Turrets

My next big wish was to see the underside of the gun barrels, and go beneath where the gun layers and aimers and those involved with the shell hoisting and handling had to operate. I was reminded that this was not a public area, nor a place which is normally opened to the public, but as I had come from the other side of the world to see the ship, I would be allowed to have a look, at my own risk.

▶ View from the wheelhouse with monument dead ahead.

▼ Wheelhouse (Travis Davis).

▲ Portside number one gun, showing shell and breech loading.

▼ Starboard number two gun, showing powder charges and shell hoist on left-hand side.

The Barbette

It is not generally appreciated that the heavily-armoured roundel of the gun barbette beneath a gun turret is the operational centre of the gun housing. In this period of ship development, the gunners sit beneath the barrels rather than beside them or behind them. It has also to be understood that these guns typically have a 4ft recoil, so that space which looks to be available is actually taken up by the barrel of the gun sliding to the aft end of the turret when the projectile is fired. Elevation also uses space in terms of having to keep clear of the arc which this requires. No wonder then that, when the gun was fired, the crew members who were not seated had to strap themselves to the side of the turret as the monster barrel moved back and forth. It is said, but I wouldn't bet on it, that the noise was not so bad inside the housing because of the effect of the armour plating on the turret giving a measure of insulation.

This kind of gun is propelled with powder cartridges. The shell is quite separate from the propellant, and both have to be loaded into the barrel in a sequential operation. It is not like small arms fire, where the cartridge is included with the shell case as one unit. Varying charges of powder were ordered for different kinds of shell, and

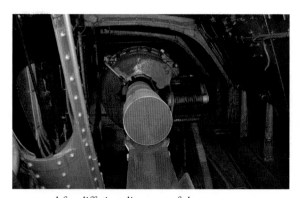

measured for differing distances of shot.

It is well beyond my brief to say more, and I am simply reporting on what I saw in front of my eyes. Somewhat similar to the engine room with all its dials, the gun aimer's position is surrounded by wheels, cylinders, gauges and pipe work, but most prominent of all is the Acme thread of the gun barrel elevation screw, which shows clearly what it takes to raise and lower a 62-ton barrel.

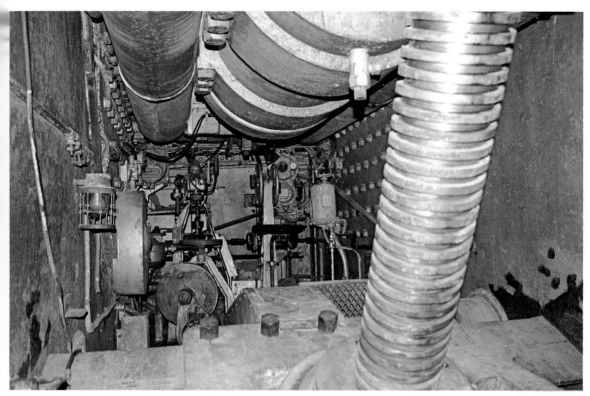

▲ Gun laying and gun aiming positions under the barrel.

▼ The breech block and hinge.

The Breech Block

The interrupted thread of the breech block shown on the starboard number two gun is an impressive piece of heavy precision engineering, closing as it must on its hinge, with perfect gas-tightness. This is one of the most skilled examples demanded of gunsmiths, which overcomes the age old problem of sealing the charge in the barrel, but being able instantly to reopen the aft end of the breech for reloading. On this gun, reloading could be achieved in forty-five seconds, but in common practice it took nearer one minute, the shells being supplied from the hoist inverted for swifter handling. The handbook mentions that twenty-five men operated the different levels of the turret, forty-five men were required to operate the magazines below, and it took seventy men to operate each turret system. There were no fatal accidents recorded of injury to the gun crews throughout the ship's long life.

The Barrels

The barrels we see today are not the original ones; they were replaced during the Second World War before the ship was called for service in the Pacific. The gun cheeks

are original, however, as witnessed by the brass label screwed into the side of the starboard cheek of number two gun (50463), recording quite clearly the date of installation as 1912, and what I believe to be the maker's initials or possibly the gun proofing mark: 'F.E.B. & B.McC.' An expert would know exactly what this denotes.

▲ The 1912 inspection plate on 14-in guns 50463.

▲ Barrel proofing marks on 5in guns.

▲ The 1911 5in gun proofing marks.

The 5in Guns

The defensive weaponry is equally well incised. The punched tooling marks record the following information: 'WNY 5in yoke, Mark VII No 2041' plus an anchor stamping and other information, which has to do with proofing and testing by the inspectorate. Very clearly and satisfyingly authentic is the date of 1911. On the very top of the breech, other stampings record what I imagine are barrel renewals or barrel testing dates in 1919, 1931 and 1942, the last being the year of my birth, which sent a shiver down my spine. The 5in guns look to be quite a handful when one considers that they would be required to fire on torpedo boats in very quick order. They may also have been altered and upgraded during their long service, particularly with regard to their pedestals and sights. What does strike me is that the slits in the casemates through which they have to fire have exactly the same limited headroom as *Thunderer*, with the sights almost scraping the armour plate above.

The Machine Shop

A final request for my long-suffering guide was to lead me to the machine shop on the third deck, again a place where you have to ask before entering. I was particularly pleased to see that the lathe had been set up with some round bar stock in the four-jaw chuck, and this was obviously a fully-working item. Even more pleasing was the restored, early electric motor, which looks like

▲ The defensive 5in gun and pedestal.

a museum piece, but is in fact contemporary with the machine. Whether or not this is of First or Second World War vintage is almost immaterial. A lathe like this can easily last a hundred years, and still turn out good work, and is in essence exactly what I have used to produce my model on a very much smaller scale. Here in the tool room for me was the real meeting place of repair and manufacture: a place where I felt entirely at home.

The lathe itself is a bit of a mix, as so many of them are; underneath the gearbox is the label of the Vandyck Churchill Co Machine Tools; the gearbox ratios for thread cutting are emblazoned in bronze with the American Tool Works Co, Cincinnati, USA (who are still in business). The pillar supporting the swarf tray is similarly labelled up in cast iron embossed lettering. These manufacturers expected their tools to last forever. There were many other items one would expect to see – pillar drill, indexing machine, milling machine, shaper and so forth, with which it would have been possible to make and mend almost anything from scratch within the capacity of the particular machine.

Unique Example

I am initially aware that I have only scratched the surface of this vessel. I am still amazed that it is possible to preserve a life-sized, 1912 floating battleship for what is a period of nearly a hundred years. I am respectful that successive generations of Texans have administered and looked after this ship with such enthusiasm and determination, so that others from all over the world may know what it was like to serve their country at sea. She is, in every sense, important and unique.

Reflecting on the visit to the United States in November 2008, I am glad that I was three years into the build of my own model when I visited, or I suspect that I might have been entirely overwhelmed by the prospect of tackling a major twentieth-century battleship, albeit in miniature. Seeing the real thing is about paying homage to the early twentieth-century engineers and constructors of these gargantuan, terrifying, war machines, and a respect for the men who sailed and fought in them. Neither Germany nor Great Britain has anything of the kind left to show the younger generation, and USS *Texas* is a remarkable exhibit, coming towards her own centenary in May 2012.

◀ Restored electric motor for lathe.　　　　　　　　▲ Lathe in the machine shop.

▼Quick change gear box, pitch of feed plate for thread cutting.

THE AMERICAN TOOL WORKS CO.
CINCINNATI, U.S.A.

GEARS IN STUD BOX	THD. FD.	THD. FD.	THD. FD.	THD. FD.	THD. FD.	THD. FD.	THD. FD.	THD. FD.	HANDLES
60 30	2　8	2¼　9	2½　10	2¾　11	2⅞　11½	3　12	3¼　13	3½　14	B. C.
	4　16	4½　18	5　20	5½　22	5¾　23	6　24	6½　26	7　28	A. C.
	8　32	9　36	10　40	11　44	11½　46	12　48	13　52	14　56	B. D.
	16　64	18　72	20　80	22　88	23　92	24　96	26　104	28　112	A. D.
30 60	8　32	9　36	10　40	11　44	11½　46	12　48	13　52	14　56	B. C.
	16　64	18　72	20　80	22　88	23　92	24　96	26　104	28　112	A. C.
	32　128	36　144	40　160	44　176	46　184	48　192	52　208	56　224	B. D.
	64　256	72　288	80　320	88　352	92　368	96　384	104　416	112　448	A. D.

~ Postscript ~

What Happened at Jutland?

Being a modelmaker rather than a naval historian, I am very hesitant to enter into the controversies of what happened at the Battle of Jutland. All I know is that this naval engagement was the set piece, the final theatre of war for the two opposing fleets and, because *Thunderer* played her part in this denouement, it is necessary to try and explain what happened. Much of what I hint at is a precis of the explanation given in *The Oxford Companion to Ships and the Sea* (1976), edited by Peter Kemp, but if you want to know more, then more than enough has been written up in the annals of naval warfare.

With a greatly superior number of ships, it was anticipated that Britain would win the engagement decisively. Wherever the engagement finally took place, it would be another Trafalgar, an indisputable victory which would make up for the ghastly stalemate of trench warfare on the Western Front, with which the First World War will be forever associated. The fleets were known respectively as the Grand Fleet (British) and the High Seas Fleet (German). The Grand Fleet was anchored at Scapa Flow in the Orkney Islands, north of Scotland, and the High Seas Fleet at Wilhelmshaven, sharing the same estuary coastline as the newly-dug Kiel Canal, in the area known in Britain as the German Bight.

The two fleets were organised along very similar lines. They were, in the first instance, divided into battlecruisers and destroyers, which had speed on their side, and second, following after them, fleets of battleships and cruisers to concentrate the heaviest guns on their counterparts. Battlecruisers were preceded into the battle zone by what was known as an 'advanced screen' of fast light cruisers. Vice Admiral Sir David Beatty commanded the British battlecruisers, and Vice Admiral Franz von Hipper those of the German High Seas Fleet. Likewise, the fleet of battleships were commanded by, respectively, Admiral Sir John Jellicoe, and Vice Admiral Reinhard Scheer.

It would be approaching two years after the outbreak of war on land before these two fleets met, on

▼ *Thunderer* depicted with her pre-war funnel bands; these, in varying configurations, identified individual battleships. They were removed in September 1914.

31 May 1916. Germany's fleet was not evenly matched with Britain's, so that open confrontation was not a strategy which the German commanders wished to pursue. The German plan was to use their superiority in submarine warfare, stationing their U-boats off the entrances of the British fleet bases, and then proceed to sea with the fleet up the Danish coast, hoping that this would then tempt the British fleet to sea, thus allowing the U-boats to attack with torpedoes. Bad weather hampered this plan, and it was only on 30 May that the weather allowed the German fleet to sail.

It seems astounding, with all the communications technology available to both sides, that neither of the two advancing forces of battlecruisers, nor the advanced screen of light cruisers, knew exactly where their opponents were. Neither spotter planes, balloons, Zeppelins, nor even submarines, had signalled the whereabouts of the two fleets, although the aviator Rutland had spotted the German light cruisers from his Short Bros 184 two-seater seaplane at 3.31pm, and his observer sent no less than four encoded wireless messages to the aircraft carrier *Engadine*, stating that he had seen enemy cruisers heading north-west. Three of these messages were received by *Engadine*, but there was a ban on ship-to-ship wireless transmission, and attempts to relay the vital information by searchlight to Beatty failed. Lacking any sightings of the enemy by the late afternoon, both sides considered turning back. It was only a Swedish merchant ship, spotted by the reconnaissance cruisers on both sides simultaneously, which finally drew attention to the whereabouts of the opposing fleets.

Without delay, Vice Admiral Beatty, with six battle-cruisers, engaged his opposite number Vice Admiral Scheer, who had command of only five battlecruisers. Fierce fighting took place, but faulty British battlecruiser design has been blamed for the loss of HMS *Indefatigable* and HMS *Queen Mary*, and occasioned the memorable retort by Beatty that 'There seems to be something wrong with our bloody ships today.' What Beatty did not know was that Admiral von Hipper, with his fleet of battleships, was steaming at full speed behind Scheer, straight for the scene of engagement. The reason Beatty did not have this vital information to hand was that the British Admiralty had signalled the misinformation that the High Seas Fleet was still in harbour. To be fair, the German forces were also uninformed, and unaware that the British battle fleet had put to sea.

Suddenly faced with the full might of Germany's

battle fleet as well as their battlecruisers, Beatty made the decision to reverse his own battlecruisers and head north, with the intention of leading the High Seas Fleet into the path of the oncoming British battleships some

eighty miles distant, but by this time the heavy engagement with the battlecruisers had led to confusion, compounded by an error in signalling which failed to make his intentions clear to other British ships.

▲ Picture taken of *Thunderer* after some hard steaming at sea – note the poor condition of the paintwork, especially along the waterline. The original tall masting system is still in place, indicating the photograph is dated *c*.1915. Photo: B Hopkins, Southsea.

The British battle fleet yet to engage with Scheer and Hipper included HMS *Thunderer* as a part of the Second Division of the Second Battle Squadron, commanded by Captain J A Ferguson RN, under the flag of Vice Admiral Sir Martyn Jerram.

The combined fleets came into contact very late in the day at about 6.00pm, eighty miles west of the coast of the Jutland Peninsula. Even at this crucial moment, Jellicoe did not know the exact position of his counterpart von Hipper. Mention of *Thunderer* comes at 6.23pm, as Massie records in *Castles of Steel* (2003): 'HMS *Iron Duke* opened fire at *Wiesbaden*; seven minutes later she found a more suitable target in one of the Königs and gave the German nine salvos. *Benbow*, *Colossus*, *Orion*, *Monarch* and *Thunderer* joined in. For the first fifteen minutes firing came from only one third of the British fleet.' *Thunderer* fired a total of thirty-seven shells, suffering no personal damage.

Jellicoe's intentions were to deploy the fleet in such

▲ Photograph taken post-war, c.1921: notice the absence of the torpedo net booms, and the nameplate fixed to the aft citadel wall. Also fitted are the automatic searchlights surrounding the aft funnel. The topmast is much reduced.

a way that he could block off the German fleet from being able to return to their home base, and in this he succeeded by crossing the 'T' of the German line of battle. Had this all happened in the middle of the day, Jellicoe would have put the British in a very strong position for decisive victory, but fog and darkness descended, leaving both fleets steaming south towards the German minefields. More erroneous information from the deciphering department of the Admiralty indicated that Scheer was making for the most northerly channel through the German minefields, but Jellicoe was convinced that he would take one of the southern routes. The result of further lack of communication to Jellicoe was that in the middle of the night

armoured cruisers and eight destroyers. German losses were one pre-dreadnought battleship, one battlecruiser, four light cruisers and five destroyers. Both nations claimed victory, but there was also an underlying sense of disappointment on both sides. The German Navy knew that the High Seas Fleet would never sail again, and serious mutinies were to follow in 1917 and 1918.

The British Navy was shown to be lacking in effective communications, particularly in signalling and transmitting information effectively. Accusations were also levelled at the design of the much vaunted battle-cruisers. These beautiful ships proved to be insufficiently armoured to prevent lethal penetration. The accuracy of British gunnery and the quality of British-made shells also came in for severe comment, but most of all, British people felt that they had been cheated and sold short. Britain had not ruled the waves. It was not the hoped-for Trafalgar; it was just an unattractive and unsatisfactory stalemate.

The positive outcome for *Thunderer* and her crew is that she survived intact and without injury, allowing her to join forces with the American Ninth Division in the latter stages of the First World War. We have also seen that the stories of the two ships interlocked in the Second World War, when *Thunderer*'s 42ft cutter played a role in the D-Day preparations, whilst *Texas* was designated as a bombardment force flagship for Omaha beach in the Western Taskforce. From approximately 3,000 yards range, and firing her main guns at

Scheer, despite a destroyer battle to the rear of the fleet, had managed to regain the advantage by crossing the stern of the Grand Fleet and slipped silently home without further loss.

British losses amounted to three battlecruisers, three

▼ Broadside picture taken after the war in 1921, when *Thunderer* was serving as a cadet training ship. Note the flying off ramps on the super-firing turrets 'B' & 'X', the shortened mast, and the modification of the extended manoeuvring compass platform, encircling the fore funnel. Photo by Gieves Ltd. Courtesy of John Hamlin.

almost nil degrees elevation, she fired upon snipers and machine gun nests. It is not always appreciated that one of the major roles of battleships is the bombardment techniques required before an invading army can make a successful assault from the beaches to the headland. Naval battles are not necessarily ship-to-ship or conducted far out at sea – also they often engage closely with the enemy's force on land. Simply put, the naval vessel is no more than a stable gun platform which can give covering fire at either very close range, or up to 10,000 yards from the target.

Thunderer herself was requisitioned as a cadet training ship in 1921, the only one of her class to escape the Washington Treaty, which claimed the lives of so many relatively new battleships. She served her country for a further five years before eventually being scrapped in 1926. Steve Woodward records that she was stripped down at Rosyth, to reduce her draft, and then finally taken apart and sold for scrap at Blyth in

Northumbria. Despite attempts to lighten her, she resisted to the last, by grounding at the entrance of the harbour, and it took just under a week to re-float her. She went to her end under her own steam, using the remaining fore funnel only.

And here we must leave her. It is a fact of life that if she had been badly stricken, or even sunk, more people would know about her, but as we come to the time of her centenary she nevertheless presents herself as the finest, and only, example of twentieth-century dreadnought shipbuilding on the river Thames, from the yard where iron shipbuilding began some fifty years before.

▼ This atmospheric watercolour by that great painter of dreadnoughts William Wyllie depicts, in the foreground, one the of the Orion class at anchor, taking on stores.

~Bibliography~

Admiralty, Lords Commissioners of, *Manual of Seamanship 1937*, Vol 1, (London, 1938).

Armstrong, Richard, *Powered Ships: The Beginnings* (London, 1974).

Attwood, Edward L, *War-Ships: A text-book on construction, protection, stability, turning, etc, of war vessels* (London, 1906).

Ballantine, Stuart, *Radio Telephony for Amateurs* (Philadelphia, 1922).

Brown, David K, *The Grand Fleet: Warship Design and Development 1906-22* (London, 1999).

Bruce, J M, *Short 184,* Windsock Datafile 85 (Berkhamsted, 2001).

Burns, Ian M, *Ben my Chree, Woman of My Heart: Isle of Man Packet Steamer and Seaplane Carrier* (Leicester, 2008).

Croydon, Air Commodore Bill, *Early Birds: A Short History of How Flight Came to Sheppey* (Sheppey, 2006).

Davis, Mick, *Sopwith Aircraft* (Marlborough, 1999).

Guttman, Jon, *Sopwith Camel vs Fokker Dr1: Western Front 1917-18* (Oxford, 2008).

Hore, Peter, *The World Encyclopedia of Battleships* (London, 2007).

Jane, Fred T, *The World's Warships 1915* (London, 1915).

Jane's All The World's Aircraft 1919, reprint edited and compiled by C G Grey (Newton Abbot, 1969).

Kemp, Peter, *The Oxford Companion to Ships and the Sea* (Oxford, 1976).

Lavery, Brian, *Ship* (London, 2004).

McAuley, Rob, and Ian Johnston, *The Battleships* (London, 2002).

Massie, Robert K, *Dreadnought: Britain, Germany, and the Coming of the Great War* (London, 1993).

—, *Castles of Steel: Britain, Germany, and the Winning of the Great War at Sea* (London, 2004).

May, W E, *The Boats of Men-of-War* (Chatham, 2003).

Milne, Graeme J, *North East England 1850-1914: The Dynamics of a Maritime Industrial Region* (Woodbridge, 2006).

Nares, Lieut George S, *Seamanship* (1862, 2nd edition), facsimile reprint with an introduction by David R Macgregor (Woking, 1979).

Nares, Vice Admiral Sir George S, *Seamanship* (7th edition) (Portsmouth, 1897).

Paasch, Capt H, *Illustrated Marine Encyclopedia* (1890), facsimile reprint with an introduction by David Macgregor (Watford, 1977).

Pears, Cdr Randolph, *British Battleships 1892-1957* (London, 1957).

Pinchbeck, Neil, 'Jutland: A Short Story', *Scale Aviation Modeller*, November 2005.

Preston, Antony, *Aircraft Carriers* (Greenwich, Connecticut, 1991).

Roberts, John, *The Battleship Dreadnought* (London, 2001).

Robertson, Bruce, *Sopwith: The Man and His Aircraft* (London, 1970).

Sothern, J W M, *"Verbal" Notes and Sketches for Marine Engineers: A Manual of Marine Engineering Practice* (12th edition, London, nd).

Thetford, Owen, *British Naval Aircraft 1912-1958* (London, 1958).

Thomas, Roger D, and Brian Patterson, *Dreadnoughts in Camera 1905-1920* (Stroud, 1998).

Wells, Captain John, *The Immortal Warrior: Britain's First and Last Battleship* (Emsworth, 1987).

Woodward, Steve, 'Orion Class Battleship – HMS *Thunderer*', 23 October 2007, http://www.shipsnostalgia.com/guides/Orion_class_battleship-_HMS_Thunderer

~List of Suppliers~

Alec Tiranti: silcone rubber, sculptor's supplies, low-melt metals, Chavant, casting centrifuge, herculite. www.tiranti.co.uk

Axminster Power Tools: spring clamps, miniature ratchet grip/bar, hand clamps, Lie Neilson round-faced spokeshave, universal work holder engraving vice, Kumagoro Japanese draw saw. www.axminster.co.uk

BECC: lettering, draught markings. www.becc.co.uk

Chatham Historic Dockyard: scale models. www.chdt.org.uk

De Walt: radial arm saw, bandsaw DW100. www.dewalt.co.uk

Dockyard Model Company: miniature chisels (1.5mm and 2mm) and gouges. PO Box 108, Florissant, CO80816, USA

Dolls House Emporium: junction board. www.dollshouse.com

Dremel: sander/linisher, drill and stand. www.dremeleurope.com

Eclipse: hacksaw. www.toolventure.co.uk

Fred Aldous: pewter sheet, copper sheet. www.fredaldous.co.uk

Futaba: radio control (six-channel). www.futaba-rc.com

Hegner UK: scroll saw (multi-cut one). www.hegner.co.uk

James Lane Display Models: guard rails. 30 Broadway, Blyth, Northumberland NE24 2PP

K&S Metals: brass tubing. www.ksmetals.com

Liberon: French (button) polish. www.liberon.co.uk

Maidstone Engineering: brass bar. www.maidstone-engineering.co.uk

Maun: pliers. www.maun-industries.co.uk

Myford: Super 7B lathe. www.myford.com

National Maritime Museum: scale models, plans. www.nmm.ac.uk

Pebeo: Setacolor fabric paint. www.pebeo.com

Perma-Grit Tools: square diamond-coated file. www.permagrit.com

Picreator Enterprises: Renaissance wax. www.picreator.co.uk

Proxxon: milling machine, belt sander. www.proxxon-direct.com

Punctilio Model Spot: decking timber. www.modelspot.com

Record Power Tools: block hand plane. www.recordpower.co.uk

Rotring: drawing board. www.rotring.com

Science Museum: scale models. www.sciencemuseum.org.uk

Scientific Wire Co: copper wire. www.wires.co.uk

Shesto: needle flame (propane gas) by Sievert Classic torch system. www.shesto.co.uk

Titebond: aliphatic wood glue. www.titebonduk.com

Tracy Tools: engineer's slitting saws, 4BA tap for light fitting. www.tracytools.com

Weller Soldering: 100 soldering iron. www.wellersoldering.com

X-Acto: razor saw. www.xacto.com